IRON WOMEN

The Ladies Who Helped Build the Railroad

CHRIS ENSS

TWODOT®

GUILFORD, CONNECTICUT
HELENA, MONTANA

A · TWODOT® · BOOK

An imprint and registered trademark of The Rowman & Littlefield Publishing Group, Inc.
4501 Forbes Blvd., Ste. 200
Lanham, MD 20706
www.rowman.com

Distributed by NATIONAL BOOK NETWORK

British Library Cataloguing in Publication Information available

Library of Congress Cataloging-in-Publication Data

Names: Enss, Chris, 1961– author.
Title: Iron women : the ladies who helped build the railroad / Chris Enss.
Description: Guilford : TwoDot, 2020. | Includes bibliographical references
    and index. | Summary: "A history of the contributions women made to the
    building of the US railroad system"— Provided by publisher.
Identifiers: LCCN 2020033417 (print) | LCCN 2020033418 (ebook) | ISBN
    9781493037759 (paperback) | ISBN 9781493037766 (epub)
Subjects: LCSH: Railroads—United States—History—19th century. |
    Women—United States—History—19th century.
Classification: LCC HE2751 .E67 2020 (print) | LCC HE2751 (ebook) | DDC
    385.092/520973—dc23
LC record available at https://lccn.loc.gov/2020033417
LC ebook record available at https://lccn.loc.gov/2020033418

♾ The paper used in this publication meets the minimum requirements of American National Standard for Information Sciences—Permanence of Paper for Printed Library Materials, ANSI/ NISO Z39.48-1992.

CONTENTS

ACKNOWLEDGMENTS

With a deep sense of gratitude, the author expresses her appreciation of the help given her by a number of interested women and men, among them being:

Claire Phillips at the California State Railroad Museum Library and Archives Department in Sacramento, California.

The Research Department at the Nevada County Historical Society in Nevada City, California.

The staff at the Nevada County Railroad Museum in Nevada City, California.

The archivists at *Harper's Magazine.*

The Society of California Pioneers.

Iris Hanney at Accessible Archives.

Mary Mathias at the National Academy of Engineering.

The staff at the Kansas Historical Society.

Paul Nelson at the National Railroad Museum in Green Bay, Wisconsin.

The staff at the Union Pacific Railroad Museum in Council Bluffs, Iowa.

The staff at the Baltimore and Ohio Railroad Museum in Baltimore, Maryland.

Stuart Rosebrook, editor for *True West* magazine.

And finally, to Erin Turner, editorial director at Rowman and Littlefield. I'm grateful beyond words for her continual support and encouragement.

Two women in front of locomotive #4 COURTESY OF THE CALIFORNIA STATE RAILROAD
MUSEUM LIBRARY & ARCHIVES

INTRODUCTION

When the last spike was hammered into the steel track of the Transcontinental Railroad on May 10, 1869, at Promontory Summit, Utah, Western Union lines sounded the glorious news of the railroad's completion. At 2:45 p.m. on that day, the following dispatch was received at New York:

Promontory Summit, Utah, May 10 – The last rail is laid! The last spike is driven! The Pacific Railroad is complete! The point of junction is 1086 miles west of the Missouri River, and 690 miles east of Sacramento City.[1]

For more than five years, an estimated four thousand men, mostly Irish working west from Omaha and Chinese working east from Sacramento, moved like a vast assembly line toward the end of the track.[2] Editorials in newspapers and magazines from coast to coast praised the accomplishment, and some boasted that the work "was begun, carried on, and completed solely by men." The August 1869 edition of *Godey's Lady's Book and Magazine* reported, "No woman has laid a rail; no woman has made a survey." The article added that

the muscular force and the intellectual guidance have come alike from men. It is worthwhile for the women who are clamoring for the suffrage to reflect whether the right to vote does not imply a capacity for the hard work of subduing the world, mental and physical, to which so far only men have been found competent.

We have indicated again and again in this publication what we believe to be the true sphere of woman: in the home, in society, among the poor; refining and ennobling social intercourse; alleviating the misery of the world. She can do these things now; if she contests man's work with him, she can do them no longer. Not by her hand can build the city . . . or the railroad.[3]

Although the physical task of building the railroad had been achieved by men, women made significant and lasting contributions to the historic operation. The female connection with railroading dates as far back as 1838, when women were hired as registered nurses/stewardesses in passenger cars. Those ladies attended to the medical needs of travelers and acted as hostesses of sorts, helping passengers have a comfortable journey.

Susan Morningstar was one of the first women on record employed by a railroad. She and her sister, Catherine Shirley, were hired by the Baltimore and Ohio Railroad in 1855 to keep the interior of the cars clean and orderly. The feminine, homey touches they added to the railroad car's décor attracted female travelers and transformed the stark, cold interior into a more welcoming setting.[4]

Miss E. F. Sawyer became the first female telegraph operator when she was hired by the Burlington Railroad in Montgomery, Illinois, in 1872. The following year, Union Pacific Railroad executives followed suit by hiring two women to be telegraph operators in Kansas City, Missouri.[5]

Inventress Eliza Murfey focused on the mechanics of the railroad, creating devices for improving the way bearings on the rail wheel attached to train cars responded to the axles. The device, or packing as it was referred to, was used to lubricate the axles and bearings. Murfey held sixteen patents for her 1870 invention.[6]

In 1879, another woman inventor named Mary Elizabeth Walton developed a system that deflected emissions from the smokestacks on railroad locomotives. She was awarded two patents for her pollution-reducing device.[7]

A cattle rancher's daughter, Nancy P. Wilkerson, from Terre Haute, Indiana, created the cattle car in 1881. Using a rack-and-pinion mechanism, she devised sliding partitions that separated the livestock from the food compartments and water troughs.[8]

From the mechanical to the ornamental and a combination of both, women like civil engineer Olive Dennis and architect Mary Colter made their marks on the railroad in the late 1890s. While employed with the Baltimore and Ohio, Olive introduced reclining passenger seats and individual window vents that not only allowed fresh air into the car but

Women played a significant role in shaping the American railroad. Many worked in machine shops welding and sorting washers. CALIFORNIA STATE RAILROAD MUSEUM LIBRARY AND ARCHIVES

also trapped dust. The refinements were quickly adopted by railroad lines across the country.

Mary Colter was the chief architect and decorator for the Fred Harvey Company. Harvey developed the Harvey House restaurants and hotels that served rail passengers on the Atchison, Topeka and Santa Fe Railway. Mary designed and decorated Harvey's eateries and inns. She considered the La Posada Hotel in Winslow, Arizona, to be her finest work.

In addition to Mary Colter's architecture and decorating style, Fred Harvey's establishments were further enhanced by the "attractive and intelligent young women of good character" who worked at his eating houses throughout the West. Dressed in their starched black-and-white shirts, bibs, and aprons, the always beautiful Harvey Girls served cowhands, trainmen, and travelers from Dodge City, Kansas, to Santa Fe, New Mexico.

"The girls at a Fred Harvey place never look dowdy, frowsy, tired, slip-shot or overworked," an article in the June 22, 1905, edition of the *Leavenworth Times* noted. "They are expecting you—clean collars, clean aprons, hands and faces washed, nails manicured—there they are bright, fresh, healthy, and expectant."[9]

Two of the most desirous locations Harvey Girls sought to work were the Cardenas Hotel in Trinidad, Colorado, and the El Garces in Needles, California. Both were beautifully situated and uniquely designed. The El Garces was referred to as the "crown jewel" of the entire Fred Harvey chain.

Soiled doves capitalized on the business opportunities the completed railroad line introduced. Ambitious madams acquired their own cars and transformed the interiors into parlor houses. Independently contracted locomotives would transport the rolling houses of ill repute and the wicked women aboard to various cow towns along the Southern Pacific Railroad.

Highly principled ladies were able to make just as much of a fortune from the railways as disreputable women. Sarah Clarke Kidder, the first female railroad president, proved women were just as capable of running a rail line as men. In 1901, Sarah took over as head of California's Nevada County Narrow Gauge Railroad. The rail line, which hauled lumber, farm produce, and gold destined for the United States Mint in San Francisco, flourished during her twelve-year rule.

Cora Mears Pitcher took over as president of the short line, the Silverton Northern Railroad, in southwest Colorado in 1931. Her father, Otto Mears, built the railway in 1885 to support the lucrative mining business in the area. The Silverton Northern Railroad ran from Silverton up the Animas River to Eureka. Cora took great pride in assuming responsibility for the line and in preserving the memory of her father, who also had operated a successful copper mine in the region.

Stage actress Lillie Langtry, one of the most famous actresses of the time, made traveling by rail a glamorous experience. The interior of her private car, called the LaLee, featured upholstered seats, admirably carved woodwork inlaid with silver bands, plush carpeting, and a ceiling of diamond-shaped form on a lightly tinted lavender background. In 1904, Lillie and LaLee traveled to Val Verde County, Texas, to meet the well-known justice of the peace Judge Roy Bean. The judge was a great admirer of Lillie's and had written her several times expressing his devotion. Sadly, the judge passed away before the actress's visit.

Popular playwright and actress Eleanor Robson Belmont also traveled across the country in her own private car. Velvet curtains and a crystal chandelier adorned her palatial suite. "A private railroad car is not an acquired taste," she told a reporter with the *San Francisco Call Chronicle Examiner* in 1906. "One takes to it immediately."[10]

Publisher and author Miriam Leslie might have done more to promote traveling by rail than any other woman in the nineteenth century. In 1877, she embarked on an extravagant five-month train trip from New York to San Francisco. Onboard the Union Pacific, she visited such popular western locations as Salt Lake City, Utah; Cheyenne, Wyoming; and Denver, Colorado. Miriam referred to the ride across the frontier as "exhilarating" and looked forward to seeing every square mile of the popular towns and cities on the itinerary.

"Wyoming was like a new world. No wilder or more grandly, lonely landscape has yet unfolded," Miriam wrote. "Going to sleep in Cheyenne we awoke in Denver, our car having been attached during the night to a train upon the Denver Pacific Railroad. Denver lies broadly and generously upon a great plain sloping toward the South Platte, with the grand sweep of the Rocky Mountain chain almost surrounding it. A large number of handsome houses have been built on the western side of the city, facing the mountain view; and one foresees when Denver is forty instead of twenty years old, this will be the fashionable and charming quarter."[11]

Besides the Denver Pacific Railroad, Miriam enjoyed numerous treks on other short line railways like the Virginia and Truckee Railroad, which connected to the Central Pacific. "There is a rise of 1,700 feet from Carson to Virginia City from whither we were bound, and the train winds heavily up between mountain walls of dust-brown rock," the vivacious author wrote of her journey through Nevada. "Not a tree, shrub, herb, nor blade of grass grew. There was nothing with life or motion in it except the brawling Carson River which plunged magnificently down between these mountains on even a steeper grade than the road winds up. What a daunting view!"[12]

Miriam contributed articles about the trip in *Frank Leslie's Illustrated Newspaper*, a popular publication she co-owned with her husband. She also wrote a book about the journey titled *A Pleasure Trip from Gotham to the Golden Gate*. Miriam described in glowing terms the many scenes she passed en route from New York to California and served as a travel guide to readers coast to coast. The transcontinental tour cost more than twenty thousand dollars.

Women inspired to embark on a railroad journey after reading *A Pleasure Trip from Gotham to the Golden Gate* were required to follow several rules for the trip. According to the *Ladies' Book of Etiquette*, women were to be punctual and dress in plain, dignified clothing. They were to carry nothing more than a traveling satchel, or a fashionable carpetbag if staying overnight. The carpetbag was to contain grooming items, a mirror, reading material, crackers or a sandwich, a large shawl, night clothes, and a woolen or silk nightcap. Women were to sit quietly and not fidget. Such behavior was cited as a sure indication that she was either ill-bred or ill at ease in society.[13]

The appalling behavior of a giddy, mail-order bride and her groom was the subject of much talk when they boarded the Union Pacific Railroad in Riverside, California, in 1886 heading to San Francisco. An article in the *Riverside Daily Press* on July 10 reported that the blissful couple were fawning over each other so much that their fellow passengers complained.

"Now what's the use of it? When a couple get married and go off on a bridal tour, why so misbehave themselves as to be 'spotted' by every man, woman, and child on the train for 'fresh fish?'" the story read. "How silly the thing must appear to them when they look back after a period of six months. Are we fools when in love, and are we idiots when we marry?"[14]

A baggage man scolded the mail-order newlyweds, but they only held on to one another more tightly. Four of the women aboard formed a committee and promised to take the matter to the legislature if the railroad company could not protect its passengers from rude behavior. The

Ceremony at "wedding of the rails," May 10, 1869, at Promontory Point, Utah LIBRARY OF CONGRESS

conductor came to speak to the women and asked them not to hold what had happened against him or the railroad.[15]

"Well, the long and short of the matter was the passengers rode 150 miles wishing they had not gotten on the train, and resolving that the thing would never happen again—never," the *Riverside Daily Press* article continued. "The women all agreed that they would walk first."[16]

Whether mail-order bride or machinist, women influenced the American railroad industry. Women also performed a variety of duties from clerical to brake cleaner. They provided services essential to the efficiency and effectiveness of the business and transformed the railways from an industrial tool of hauling material and equipment to a refined means of travel.

CHAPTER I

The Telegraphers

TWENTY-EIGHT-YEAR-OLD ELIZABETH COGLEY SAT AT A SMALL DESK in the Pennsylvania Railroad ticket office in Lewiston Junction, Pennsylvania, on April 16, 1861, frantically writing down the message coming through the telegraph. The neatly dressed woman wore a serious expression; the message she was transcribing was vital and history making. The day before, a similar wire had reached Elizabeth. She carefully noted its contents and passed it along to the ranking military official in the area. It was from President Abraham Lincoln, and it read, "I appeal to all loyal citizens to favor, facilitate, and aid this effort to maintain the honor, the integrity, and the existence of our National Union, and the perpetuity of popular government; and to redress the wrongs already long enough endured." This was Lincoln's first call for troops. He asked for seventy-five thousand volunteers.[1]

The following day, Pennsylvania's first war governor, Andrew G. Curtin, sent a telegram to Captain Selheimer, commander of the First Defenders Association in Lewiston, to rally his men together to report to Harrisburg, Pennsylvania, as soon as possible. After delivering the message to the captain, Elizabeth was instructed to respond to Governor Curtin with news that he and his troops would "move at once." The railroad telegrapher dispatched the important information quickly and accurately. Little did Elizabeth know the event would be remembered as the first telegraph exchange of the Civil War.[2]

Born on November 24, 1833, Elizabeth learned telegraphy in the office of the National Telegraph Company. She entered the service of the Pennsylvania Railroad Company on April 13, 1856. She was stationed in

Elizabeth Cogley, one of the first recorded
women to work as a railroad telegrapher
AUTHOR'S COLLECTION

the Lewiston office until the beginning of the Civil War. She remained
with the railroad company for more than forty years.[3]

Some of the earliest women in railroading could be found in telegraph stations. The job of the telegrapher was to transfer information
between the train dispatcher and the train operator. A telegrapher copied
train orders and messages from the train crew and reported the passing trains to the dispatcher. They also received and sent Western Union
telegrams. Most learned the trade from another operator. Some attended
schools such as the Cooper Union for the Advancement of Science and
Art in New York and the Pittsburgh Female College in Pittsburgh.[4]

The qualifications needed to be a telegrapher were to be well read,
to know how to spell, and to be able to learn Morse code. According

to author Virginia Penny's book written in 1870 titled *How Women Can Make Money*, a good lady telegraphist could make between three hundred and five hundred dollars a year. With that in mind, many women with some knowledge of electricity and good penmanship decided to pursue a career in the field.[5]

In the beginning, a woman's presence in the railroad telegraph office was not readily accepted by the public at large. The common perception was that the job was too difficult for women to handle. Rail lines were persuaded to challenge the notion as rail stations increased across the country and more telegraphers were needed. Not only were there women willing to fill the open positions, but also railroad executives found they could get away with paying women less to do the job than men.[6]

The average work day for a lady telegrapher was more than ten hours long. The location of the telegraph offices could be difficult to handle as well. A number of the train stations where the telegraph offices were located were in desolate spots along the line. Alone for days with just the electromagnetic telegraph apparatus, operators struggled with the isolation. The job could be dangerous, too. If the equipment was not properly grounded, an operator ran the risk of being electrocuted. Such was the case with Lizzie Clapp on July 11, 1876. The eighteen-year-old woman was the operator for the Boston and Providence Railroad at Readville, Massachusetts. She was sitting at her desk, staring at a storm rolling through, when a bolt of lightning struck the telegraph wire leading to the station. The strong current traveled through the open wires to the gold necklace Lizzie was wearing. She fell to the floor dead.[7] Shortly after Lizzie's passing, steps were taken to address safety issues in telegraph offices across the country.[8]

⟋⟍

Among the other occupational hazards associated with being a telegraph operator in the late nineteenth century was the possibility of contracting tuberculosis. The long hours on the job were oftentimes spent in offices that were poorly ventilated. Contacting someone in the office who had tuberculosis was problematic because poorly ventilated buildings allowed the disease to incubate. The water supply in rural areas where stations

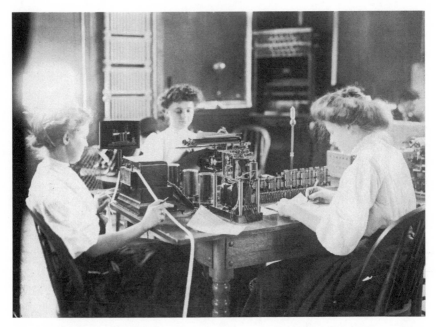

Women telegraph operators sending, receiving, and translating messages LIBRARY OF CONGRESS

were located was the source of sickness as well. Some operators contracted typhoid fever after drinking contaminated water.[9]

For many women, the advantages of being a telegraph operator far outweighed the drawbacks associated with the position. Catherine "Cassie" Tomar-Hill, telegraph operator for the Southern Pacific Railroad in Placer County, California, considered the job a blessing. Cassie came west from Iowa in 1859 in a covered wagon with her family. The Tomars eventually settled in northern California, where Cassie's father worked as a miner. In 1876, Cassie married George Washington Hill. George, a native of New York, had come west with his family when he was a young boy. The Hills ran a grocery store in Auburn, California.[10]

According to the April 30, 1999, edition of the *Press Tribune*, Cassie and George moved to Vina, California, where George had been hired as a railroad agent and telegraph operator for the Southern Pacific. Cassie learned the job of telegrapher while maintaining their modest home.[11]

Within the first five years of their marriage, the couple returned to Placer County, California, and George took over the Roseville depot and became the station's telegraph operator. In addition to his duties as telegraph operator and railroad agent, George became the Wells Fargo and Company's representative in Roseville.[12]

The family lived at the railroad depot with their five children. Cassie would assist George in sending and receiving messages over the telegraph. When George died unexpectedly in 1883, Cassie was appointed the Wells Fargo agent. At the time of her appointment, Roseville was a small agriculture town with about four hundred people. It sat at the junction of the Central Pacific and California Central Railroads, which ran from Folsom to Lincoln.[13] While serving as the Wells Fargo agent, Cassie faced the challenges of holding down her job while raising her children alone. She remained at her post as a railroad telegrapher and Wells Fargo agent for twenty-three years until her retirement on March 1, 1907.[14]

Women proved to not only be able to adequately handle the job of telegraph operator, but, in the case of Abbie Gail Struble, to be more than capable of tackling the dangers that occasionally arose with the position. Abbie and her sister, Madge, were employed as operators by the Baltimore and Ohio Railroad in 1862 and worked at a station in Allegheny, Pennsylvania, called Port Penny.[15] One bitter cold winter's evening, Abbie received a message that a locomotive pulling a single car had thundered out of Pittsburgh carrying a load of Union Army officers bound for Washington, DC, and an emergency conference called by President Lincoln. At the same time, a west-bound freight train pulled into a depot fifteen miles east of Port Perry. The conductor of the west-bound train entered the telegraph office and asked for track clearance to Pittsburgh. The message was relayed to the train dispatcher, and the "all clear" reply came back.[16]

All was as it should be until the freight train left the depot heading toward Port Perry. As it continued along its way, it picked up steam. A frantic message came through the telegraph from the train dispatcher who had issued the "all clear." "Stop that freight!" the dispatcher's message read. "There's a special train bound for Washington heading into it."

Abbie was the telegraph operator on duty who translated the dispatcher's plea. She immediately leapt into action.[17] Abbie peered out the station window and saw she had only seconds to act. There were no signals at that time to flash a warning. She raced into the freezing night just as the oncoming freight was passing and lurched toward the grab iron (or handhold) of a boxcar. She hung on, kicking frantically as she jerked about. The frosted rungs and frozen iron running bars along the top of the cars stripped the wool from her mittens as she stumbled and crawled toward the locomotive and an unsuspecting crew.[18]

Reaching the coal car, she was knocked back by a blow to the leg by the knotted end of a rope swing from a tunnel entrance. She managed to get to her feet again and attract the attention of the train's crewman shoveling coal into the furnace. Once she let the crewman know the problem, he brought the train to a stop and quickly threw the train into reverse. The crisis was averted, and the freight crew was eternally grateful to Abbie for her heroic actions.[19]

Abbie Struble was born in Montgomery County, Pennsylvania, on April 22, 1845. She and her sister, Madge, were two of the first women telegraphers to learn to receive messages by sound rather than by sight. The early telegraphers deciphered the dots and dashes of Morse code stamped onto paper strips. The ability to translate the sound of the Morse code being tapped out was crucial for routing trains quickly. It took time to convert the code stamped onto paper strips to the actual words. Being able to hear the code as it was transmitted and promptly relay the message was much more efficient.[20]

On May 24, 1866, Abbie married John Vaughan. John was a telegraph lineman who learned from his wife how to operate a telegraph by sound. The couple moved a lot during their marriage, working for rail lines from the Texas and Pacific to the Mexican National Railroad. The Vaughans had five children, all of whom worked as telegraph operators at one time or another. The family eventually settled in Long Beach, California, where Abbie taught telegraphy at a local school. She retired in 1913 but was persuaded to go back to work in 1917, when the United States entered World War I. There was a shortage of trained telegraphers, and Abbie was called upon to teach the profession to recruits.[21]

Recognized all over the country as "Mother Vaughan," Abbie passed away in the summer of 1924 at the age of seventy-nine.[22]

—◆—

Jane Denny McDowell was a skilled telegraph operator with famous ties. She was married to composer Stephen Foster and was the subject of the song "Jeanie with the Light Brown Hair." Jane was born in Pittsburgh in 1829. Her father, Dr. Andrew McDowell, was one of the city's leading physicians. She was the second in a family of six daughters. In her girlhood, she was a renowned beauty, having a rare shade of hair with eyes almost matching that attracted attention everywhere.[23]

Jane was nineteen when she married the promising songwriter. Foster was employed as an accountant. He abandoned the accounting business in 1850 and moved to New York. His ambition was to support himself and his bride with his music. His gift for harmony and poetry led to the creation of such well-known tunes as "Camptown Races" and "My Old Kentucky Home." Although his songs were produced and well received, the couple realized very little financially for his music because Stephen did not demand proper compensation from the music publishers. Multiple publishers often printed their own competing editions of his songs, paying him nothing and eroding any long-term monetary benefits.[24]

Stephen and Jane's relationship suffered because of the financial issues. It did not improve with the birth of their daughter. The couple separated often, and Stephen began drinking. Jane left for good with the child when Stephen refused to give up alcohol. Jane and their daughter moved back to Pennsylvania, where Jane studied telegraphy at the Pittsburgh Female College. Shortly after graduating, she took a job with the Pennsylvania Railroad as a telegraph operator.[25]

Stephen sank into a deep depression and continued drinking. He spent all his income on alcohol, and when he ran out of money, he sold his clothes to buy more to drink. He wore rags and went days without eating. On Saturday evening, January 9, 1864, the thirty-seven-year-old man passed out in a drunken stupor in his hotel room. When he awoke, he was violently ill from liver failure, and in his weakened condition, he fell and hit his head. He died shortly thereafter. Jane returned to New York to claim her husband's body from the hospital. Nurses gave his clothes to her along with thirty-eight cents that was found in his pocket and a scrap of paper upon which he had written the words "Dear Friends and Gentle Hearts."[26]

Jane continued to work as a telegraph operator at the railroad depot in Greensburg, Pennsylvania. She eventually remarried in 1869. Jane died a tragic death in her home in January 1903. While reclining in a chair in front of an open grate, her dress caught fire. Screaming, she threw herself on her bed. The entire bed then caught on fire. Jane was seventy-four when she passed away.[27]

Mattie Kuhn rose through the telegraphy ranks to become one of the most well-known telegraph operators in the railroad's early history. She performed several heroic acts while working for the railroad, and her escapades on the job in the early 1900s reflected the difficulties women experienced in assuming such an important position.[28]

Mattie Collins Brite was born in Atascosa County, Texas, on March 1, 1880. Her parents divorced when she was seven, and she and her sister were bounced back and forth between her parents' homes until 1891, when her mother remarried. Mattie's stepfather, Daniel G. Franks, ran the Pecos Land and Cattle Company near Meyers Spring, seven miles east of the railroad station at Dryden in south-central Terrell County. Mattie's mother, Alva, managed a boardinghouse. As the house was located close to the railroad station, many of the boarders were employees of the railroad. Some were responsible for pumping water into the boilers of steam locomotives; some were station, ticket, or freight agents; and some were telegraph operators. Mattie's contact with telegraph operators was what left a lasting impression and inspired her to pursue the career.[29]

A governess provided Mattie and her sibling with their primary education. By the time she was sixteen, she had completed what little schooling had been offered and was residing in Eagle Pass, helping her mother and stepfather run the Dolch Hotel. It was there she met her first husband, a thirty-six-year-old executive with the Mexican International

Railroad named Paul Frieson. The two were married on December 23, 1896. By their second anniversary, the couple had a son. Before their third anniversary, the pair had divorced. Alone with a baby, Mattie returned to her parents' home in Eagle Pass and began the process of finding work. An acquaintance suggested she consider learning telegraphy. Mattie remembered the telegraph operators she met at her mother's boardinghouse but wasn't certain what the job entailed. She learned that a telegrapher sent and received messages using Morse code. Telegraph operators were in high demand and had the opportunity to move from place to place and job to job to achieve a higher salary.[30]

Mattie was a quick study; in a short time, she had mastered Morse code and practiced sending messages with a homemade machine. One day while she was practicing, a guest at the Dolch Hotel overheard the tapping and questioned Mattie's stepfather about it. The guest turned out to be the superintendent of telegraphers at a railroad station in New Orleans. The superintendent was informed that Mattie was learning the profession on her own. The man was impressed with her ability to grasp the code and offered to help. He arranged for Mattie to sit in the train master's office at the local railroad depot and listen to the messages handled in the telegraph office. Mattie admitted in her memoir that learning to concentrate on one wire while several others were going was difficult, but she finally managed to focus and practiced sending messages on her makeshift device. "I learned to copy figures from hearing the lottery lists being wired from New Orleans to San Francisco and the railroad work and Western Union right there in the room," Mattie noted in her biography.[31]

Mattie's first telegraphy job was in Sabinas, Mexico. The first train order she received and copied read: "August 22, 1902. No. 2 run ten minutes late Diaz to Sabinas. Signed J. F. Dickey, Supt." Mattie's average shift was twelve hours long. When she wasn't working, she was caring for her son in the modest hotel where they lived. Although she had trained and worked hard to acquire her first job, Mattie was fearful of losing the position and wouldn't even take off when she was sick. During the first month she was at Sabinas, she contracted typhoid pneumonia. She remained on the job until she collapsed. A train crew found her unconscious in her office and helped her to her bedroom.[32]

From the station in Sabinas, Mexico, she was sent to a depot in Durango, Mexico. Mattie and her son lived in a back room where she worked. It wasn't ideal, but they were together. In March 1903, Mattie joined the Order of Railroad Telegraphers (ORT) union. The union promoted professionalism, negotiated for higher wages, and demanded better working conditions. The chairman of the Durango ORT informed Mattie he didn't want any women in his local union, but she couldn't be intimidated. Being a member of the ORT was a source of great pride for Mattie throughout her career.[33]

Mattie married a second time in late 1903, but the marriage was short-lived. She was pregnant with another son when she filed for divorce. She returned to her parents' home in Del Rio and stayed until her baby was born. Shortly after her son's birth, she went to work at the Western Union office not far from the hotel her parents operated. She learned quickly the difference between a commercial telegram and a railroad telegram. According to Mattie's autobiography, "The commercial message shows the number of words in the body of the message, in what we call the 'check'. After calling your relay office, or direct office, you give the receiver the number, each message is numbered, then the number of words in the body, meaning the message without the address, addressee, and signature." At various times in her career, Mattie worked for Western Union; however, she preferred working as a telegraph operator for the railroad. It was much more exciting to her.[34]

By 1907, Mattie was living in Austin, Texas, still working for Western Union. The superintendent at the location offered her a salary of forty dollars a month. Men doing the same job were earning sixty-five dollars a month, and Mattie knew that. When she questioned the executive on the matter, he informed her that he believed women couldn't do the job as well as men. Attempting to prove his point, he sat Mattie in front of the telegraph and challenged her to quickly copy multiple incoming messages. Mattie's abilities were recognized both by the superintendent and by the other telegraph operators working at the office. After the demonstration, Mattie's pay was set at sixty-five dollars a month.[35]

Mattie was so exceptional at her job that she was sent to work in other offices around Texas. It was a difficult venture each time because she had two children to care for and get settled. Prior to traveling to Amarillo on a ten-day assignment, a woman operator suggested she leave her boys at the Episcopal Home for Children. Mattie had misgivings but agreed to place the children in the home's care for the ten-day period. During her absence, her three-year-old son became sick with a fever. Mattie returned to find the boy's health failing rapidly. He died from an unknown illness and was buried in Oaklawn Cemetery in Dallas, Texas.[36]

Mattie's next job was at the railroad depot in Waurika, Oklahoma. She had been hired via the telegraph. She sent a message about her background to the depot agent, and he messaged her that he desperately needed an operator. He hired Mattie sight unseen. When she arrived to begin work, the agent was shocked to see his new hire was a woman. Mattie assured him she could do the job and that her gender shouldn't matter. The agent was in no position to argue the point and put her to work.[37]

A third marriage proposal came while she and her son were living in Oklahoma. Mattie accepted, but that marriage didn't last any longer than the others had. From Waurika she moved on to work at depots in El Reno, Oklahoma; Kansas City, Missouri; Leavenworth, Kansas; and St. Paul, Minnesota. In 1910, she signed with the Southern Pacific Railroad and was stationed at Marmarth, North Dakota. From there, Mattie worked at a station west of Marmarth called Dodge. After Dodge, there was the station on the Northern Pacific called Landslide in North Dakota, then on to a depot in Houston, Minnesota Falls, back to North Dakota to Grand Forks, and on to Rosebud and Helena, Montana.[38]

Telegraph operators who changed jobs as frequently as Mattie did were called *boomers*. Every job she took added to her rich experience in the field.[39]

No matter how extensive her work history, Mattie continually encountered shortsighted managers who refused to hire women. She was greeted by such a man when she reported for work for the Oregon Short Line in Pocatello, Idaho.[40]

"I arrived there about seven in the morning," Mattie recalled in her memoir, "and went directly to the telegraph office, and when the manager, A. W. Stoker, came to the counter I told him I had come to relieve Operator Fitzsimmons. Stoker's eyes bulged out and he almost swallowed his tongue. 'Why you can't work here,' he said. 'We don't hire women!' I said to him, 'You may not, but your superintendent did.'" Once the matter was settled, Mattie was allowed to do the job she was hired to do.[41]

While working in Tulare County, California, between 1911 and 1912, the chief operator asked Mattie to travel to Sacramento, the state capital, to protest the eight-hour law for women. Mattie was taken aback by the request. The idea of protesting legislature that would benefit women didn't sit well with her. She quit and went to work for the Western Pacific Railroad at a station in Gerlach, Nevada, one hundred miles west of Winnemucca, Nevada. An appendicitis attack took her out of commission for a time. She recuperated at her parents' home in Texas, and as soon as she was back on her feet, she was on the move again. This time Mattie traveled to Canada to work for the Canadian Pacific Railroad. From Canada she went to Sacramento and then to Marshfield, Oregon, and on to Austin, Nevada.[42]

On July 5, 1916, Mattie signed on again with the Southern Pacific Railroad and assumed a permanent position as telegraph operator at a station in Sparks, Nevada. Her son, now fifteen years old, was hired by the rail line to maintain the signals at Parran, Nevada, seventy-six miles away from his mother.

In 1926, Mattie became reacquainted with Albert Kuhn, a telegraph operator she had met in 1891 at her parents' boardinghouse in Texas. He was working at a station in Placer County, California, and heard her voice on the telephone repeating train orders. Albert asked if the voice belonged to Mattie, and when it was confirmed it was her voice, he sent her a message. After a lengthy courtship, the two married on May 2, 1931.[43]

Mattie and Albert lived happily for more than a year. The couple purchased land in Reno and were making plans for a long life together in northern Nevada. On February 27, 1933, Albert had a heart attack while on the job. He was taken to a hospital in San Francisco and died four days later. Several weeks later, Mattie returned to work at a station in Fernley, Nevada. Mattie retired in 1942, after forty years as a telegraph operator. Mattie wrote a book about her life and work that was printed in the April, May, and June issues of *Railroad Magazine* in 1950. Mattie Kuhn passed away in July 1971 at the age of ninety-one in Reno.[44]

The telegraphers played a significant role in the history of the railroad. They were essential for increasing traffic on single-track railroad lines, communicating the train's arrival and departure, and making the movement of people and goods safe. Skilled women operators proved they were just as capable as men to transmit the messages necessary to make operation along the railroad lines efficient.[45]

CHAPTER 2

Sarah Kidder: The Railroad President

THE NEVADA COUNTY NARROW GAUGE RAILROAD OPERATED AS IT usually did on April 10, 1901. It ran as though nothing out of the ordinary had occurred. The wood-burning engine proceeded along its customary route without delay or interruption, giving no indication that the line's president and owner had passed away.[1]

John Flint Kidder had taken charge of the Nevada County Narrow Gauge Railroad in 1884. He was a construction engineer with both the vision to maintain the line and the business sense to manage it. The twenty-five-mile route connected the gold mines in northern California to the outside world. The tracks threaded the canyons and rolling countryside between Nevada City and Grass Valley and the Central Pacific main line in Colfax. The route included steep grades, two tunnels, and several trestles, the highest being ninety-five feet above the Bear River. Kidder's Narrow Gauge carried more gold (some $300 million) than any other short line in the state. He was well respected and admired by a community that owed its progress to him.[2]

Concern over the economic impact Kidder's passing would have on the area was so great, it's surprising the railroad ran at all the day he died. Business owners who benefited from the railroad worried there would be an interruption in service that would threaten their livelihood. Rumors about who would take John Kidder's place as head of the rail line did not immediately set the minds of those businessmen at ease.[3]

John Kidder's widow, Sarah, was aware there were those who doubted she was the right one to assume control of the Narrow Gauge Railroad, but she was determined to prove she was up to the task. Less than a

Sarah Kidder, president of the Nevada County Narrow Gauge Railroad; her daughter, Beatrice; and husband, John Flint Kidder SEARLS
HISTORICAL LIBRARY AND N.C.N.C.R.R. TRANSPORTATION MUSEUM

month after her husband's death, stockholders chose Sarah as John's suc-
cessor. According to an article in the September 20, 1901, edition of the
Oakdale Leader, when Sarah Kidder accepted the job "she had the distinc-
tion of being one of the very few women, if not the only one, who ever
held such a bona fide position and title."[4]

Sole ownership of the railroad was left to Sarah, but that didn't auto-
matically mean she would be the candidate the board of directors would

select to manage it. She earned the right to do the work because, for more than a year prior to John Kidder's death, Sarah went through the process of familiarizing herself with the business affairs of the company. The *Oakdale Leader* article of September 20, 1901, noted that "Mrs. Kidder is not the sort of a woman who desired to taste the duties and responsibilities that usually fall to men."[5] Certainly, when Sarah and John were married in 1874, she did not foresee being without her husband and becoming the head of a railroad line.

Sarah was fifty-nine when she became the president of the Nevada County Narrow Gauge Railroad. She'd spent the bulk of her married life in Grass Valley, California, in an ornate, three-story mansion not far from the rail yard where her husband's office was located.[6] Prior to John's death, Sarah's focus was maintaining the family home. She had a passion for gardening and flowers, and she decorated the exterior of the house with roses of every kind. The Kidder mansion was the setting of many social events in the county, and Sarah was considered to be a most charming hostess. A number of politicians, including the governor of the state, celebrated authors, and well-known athletes spent time at the Kidder residence.[7]

Sarah and John had no children of their own, but they did have a niece named Beatrice whom they adopted. When Sarah wasn't busy taking care of the home and entertaining, she and Beatrice spent time together visiting friends in the neighborhood. If John hadn't passed away, she would have been content to be a mother and maintain the Kidder mansion.[8]

Being around the railroad business for so long, Sarah had a working knowledge of the business and was mindful of the fact that she needed to surround herself with individuals who were experts in the field. She chose her husband's right-hand man, Charles P. Loughridge, as the general manager of the line as well as three additionally respected executives to serve as her vice president, treasurer, and master mechanic. From the moment Sarah took over as president, she made it known to the stockholders and board of directors that she was going to run the railroad efficiently and honestly.[9]

The Nevada County Narrow Gauge Railroad was not without its problems when Sarah assumed control of the line. An electric railway company was expanding its interests and looking to connect Sacramento with the ranch land area of Marysville. Proponents for the Northern Electric Railway had hopes of taking the line into Nevada County, and if that happened, the life of the Narrow Gauge Railroad would be in serious jeopardy. They were afraid they would lose the business of average passengers, and companies depending on the Narrow Gauge to transport freight into the region might decide to transfer their accounts to Northern Electric Railway.[10]

A company called Nevada County Traction was the money behind the Northern Electric Railway. They were anxious to compete with the Nevada County Narrow Gauge Railroad and believed they could accomplish the goal best by first constructing an electric rail system through town. The electric train would take the place of stagecoaches used to transport people from the Narrow Gauge Railroad depot to destinations inside Grass Valley and Nevada City. Once Nevada County Traction felt they had become a firm fixture in the area, they would seek to buy land around the two towns, grade a rail line, and lay some track.[11]

Nevada County Traction broke ground in its electric train service for Grass Valley and Nevada City on June 5, 1901. The line was completed on September 9, 1901. It proved to be a costly venture. More than $217,000 was spent. In early 1902, the executives behind the company approached Sarah with an offer to buy the Nevada County Narrow Gauge Railroad from her. Nevada County Traction leaders thought that purchasing an existing line would be less expensive than building their own. Company stockholders believed Sarah might have discovered owning and managing a railroad to be too overwhelming and that she would be eager to sell. They were wrong. Sarah declined their offer, but it wouldn't be the last time the company tried to buy her out.

In October 1905, investors with Nevada County Traction met with Sarah to discuss the possibility again. After explaining how important Nevada County Traction had become with residents and how much their electric rail line touring cars and bus service were appreciated, former power plant owner and one of the directors of the company, John Martin, made another offer to buy the Narrow Gauge. Sarah quoted an astronomical price, one she anticipated could not be met. She was right.

The Nevada County Narrow Gauge Railroad in front of the Kidder Mansion
SEARLS HISTORICAL LIBRARY AND N.C.N.C.R.R. TRANSPORTATION MUSEUM

Martin informed her the offer was too high and attempted to negotiate, but Sarah refused to talk further about the matter.[12]

In the spring of 1906, Nevada County Traction made good on its promise to begin construction on a new rail line. It had completed a little more than a mile when the operation was brought to a halt. The San Francisco earthquake and fire of April 18, 1906, left Nevada County Traction in frail financial health. Many of the company's investors lost money and property in San Francisco as a result of the catastrophic event. By January 1908, any capital that was to be used to acquire the Narrow Gauge or forge ahead with a competing rail line was gone.[13]

In addition to holding her own against those who sought to take over her railroad, Sarah oversaw the continual changes and upgrades needed to be made to the line. In late 1908, all wood-burning locomotives needed to be modified to burn crude oil. The Interstate Commerce Commission required automatic couplers and airbrakes to be installed, as well as new safety procedures put into place to protect rail line passengers and Nevada County Narrow Gauge Railroad employees.[14]

Sarah's duties included finding new clients to add to the rail line's profitability. Among the many companies she negotiated with to bring large quantities of product into the region was Pacific Gas and Electric. In 1913, Sarah helped work out a deal with PG&E to supply the sand and gravel necessary for construction of the Lake Spaulding Dam. The dam, located on the Bear River north of Emigrant Gap, was one of several sizeable hydroelectric projects planned by the growing utility company. According to historical records about the undertaking, a few details needed to be handled before the Narrow Gauge Railroad could be ready to handle such a job.[15]

If the gravel could be loaded on standard gauge cars and pulled to Colfax, it could be transferred to the Southern Pacific's tracks without transshipment. The Narrow Gauge Railroad decided to add a third rail between Colfax and the Bear River. To facilitate the work necessary on the right-of-way between these two points, the railroad applied to the California Railroad Commission for permission to issue $500,000 of 5 percent bonds. On April 9, 1913, it was announced that the firm of Shattuck and Edinger had been granted the contract to add the third rail to the Narrow Gauge line between Colfax and the Bear River. The contractors went right to work replacing short ties along the route to the river with standard thirty-five-pound-sized rails.[16]

Business was good during Sarah Kidder's time as president of the Narrow Gauge Railroad. As a matter of fact, it was so good, she was able to pay her stockholders substantial dividends on their shares. When her husband ran the company, the highest ever paid was a 5 percent return. Newspapers, enamored by the woman railroad president west of the Rockies, reported on Sarah's strength and leadership skills. "In these last days when we are hearing a great deal about the 'gentlewoman in business' as the phrase so gracefully puts it in describing members of the fair sex who preside over the tearoom lunch booths and the like, or design marvelous 'confections' as the strange hats of the moment are called, it is interesting to note that there is one woman in the West who is not only 'in business' in the usual sense of the word, but is by way of being a great power in the financial world," an article in the February 27, 1912, edition of the *Republic* noted about Sarah. "And this, too, not because of the mere fact of millions, as in the case of Hetty Green, that lady who is even now ready to join the dance, but because she is by way of being 'railroad queen.' There seems to be no other way to describe Mrs. John F. Kidder. Mrs. Kidder is a real power in her own locale, where for some years now she has been 'pulling strings' of her little road and making it prosper."[17]

Sarah proved to be just as capable of dealing with the difficulties of running a lucrative rail line as she was the successes. When descendants of George Fletcher, owner of the general store in Grass Valley and one-time secretary of the Narrow Gauge Railroad when the line was first constructed, demanded shares in the railroad because they claimed George jointly owned shares with John Kidder, Sarah handled the situation fairly and smartly. George's son, Herbert, initially claimed he was owed 875 shares of stock; the figure changed to 1,252 shares, then settled at 2,500 shares. Sarah informed Herbert that she would be glad to divide the stock in question if he could prove his claim in writing.[18]

Insulted with her demand and eager to make Sarah surrender the stock, George Fletcher's family decided to deal with Sarah via the court system. Herbert filed a suit against Sarah and the Nevada County Narrow Gauge Railroad, claiming that both the business and the business owner "wants to defraud the George Fletcher estate." Sarah and the company launched a countersuit stating that the complaint brought by Herbert did not state facts sufficient to constitute a course of action. The court agreed with Sarah, and Herbert's claim was dismissed.[19]

In early 1907, Sarah made the bold move to add a new locomotive to the line. The new piece of equipment ran exclusively by gasoline. A new coach was added, too. It seated fifteen persons and was designed with a view to carrying mail and baggage. The new engine and coach took the place of the steam locomotive in operation and was used to connect with the Overland Limited at Colfax. It had previously been necessary to run a full train and crew to connect with the overland, and in many instances, the train had been obliged to make the run with only one or two passengers and possibly some miscellaneous baggage and freight. The new locomotive and coach would prove to be more cost efficient.[20]

One of the most significant decisions made by Sarah on behalf of the rail line occurred in 1904. The need for a bridge to be built along the route the Narrow Gauge Railroad traveled was presented to the board in a stockholders meeting by Sarah and her staff. The bridge would be a shortcut for the line, which had to travel two miles around a rocky region to get to the other side. Construction of the Bear River Bridge began in 1908. The steel bridge was 800 feet long, stood 173 feet 9 inches above the river, and cost $65,000 to build.[21]

The continued improvements implemented to the rail line further benefited the Narrow Gauge Railroad stockholders. The July 8, 1908, edition of the *San Francisco Bulletin* called attention to Sarah's management style in an article titled "Woman Runs Road":

> *Few railroads anywhere revel in a dividend of ten percent, but what makes this one really remarkable is the fact that it was earned under the direction of a woman—the only woman in all the world, perhaps, who is an active steam railroad president. This marvel of femininity, management, and finance is Mrs. S. A. Kidder of Grass Valley, California, and her line known as the Nevada County Narrow Gauge Railroad, is in the northern central part of this state.*
>
> *No figurehead is Mrs. Kidder. When, after the death of her husband, she was elected president in his stead, she found the road worn to a frazzle and in debt. Mrs. Kidder mended the roadbed, put in new rails, and purchased new rolling stock. In 1903 the line began to pay. Now it is one of the most remunerative of its size in all the land.*
>
> *Connecting Nevada City and Grass Valley with the Southern Pacific system at Colfax, it does a good freight and a considerable passenger business and is the only outlet of one of the busiest gold mining sections in the west.*
>
> *Mrs. Kidder did not seek the presidency of the Nevada County Narrow Gauge Railroad: the office sought her. When her husband died in April 1901, the stockholders and directors unanimously turned to her as his successor. Together, husband and wife had battled their way to the front through the vicissitudes that so often mark life in the mining sections of the west.*
>
> *In all of Mr. Kidder's business ventures including the management of the railroad, she had been his confidant and aid, and her*

ability as an executive was well recognized. In fact, no one else was suggested as the new head of the company, and she has been reelected each year since.

When this woman president took up the reins of management, she found that she had much to do. For eighteen years, not a dividend had been declared. Moreover, the road was in debt and its physical condition all run down. Passing through a mountainous region for much of its length, with sharp curves and heavy grades, Mrs. Kidder found that the road bed was so imperfect and the rails so light as to preclude the possibility of trains of sufficient size to pay. The rolling stock, too, had to be overhauled, renewed, and increased.

All this meant a large outlay, but Mrs. Kidder knew that sufficient business could be developed to warrant the expense. So, she procured the money and spent it. For the first time in many years, the road was equipped to handle the business offered, and then the president reached out after more business.

Aiding a systematic attempt to boom that section through widespread advertising, she also encouraged the enlargement of mining operations, the establishment of mining operations, the establishment of new cattle ranges, the planting of more and bigger orchards, and an increase in tourist travel. All this helped to put money into the treasury of the Nevada County Narrow Gauge Railroad.[22]

By the summer of 1910, Sarah's interest in the railroad had begun to wane. For more than nine years, Sarah had been focused on the Narrow Gauge. She'd chosen to be more than simply a figurehead at the company and had no regrets. She did, however, miss her adopted daughter, Beatrice; Beatrice's husband, Howard Ridgely Ward; and their infant daughter, all of whom were living in the northwest Arctic region. On June 27, 1910, Sarah decided to embark on a cruise to Alaska to visit Beatrice and her little girl. Sarah had been struggling with her health and had undergone minor surgery just prior to the trip. She believed the time away would provide her with the rest she needed as well as lift her spirits.[23]

Shortly after Sarah returned from her visit with Beatrice and her family, a rumor began circulating that she was planning to sell her shares in the railroad and retire from the business world. Although she did not readily admit she was divesting her stock, the rumors proved to be accurate. An article in the November 2, 1911, edition of the *Evening Herald* reported that "Mrs. S. A. Kidder, the Grass Valley, California, millionaire and the only woman railroad president, has disposed of her stock in the Nevada County Narrow Gauge Railroad." The report added that Sarah's plan after the sale of her stock included "travel and rest."[24]

Walter Arnstein and Samuel L. Naphtaly, president and vice president of the Oakland, Antioch and Eastern Railroad, purchased Sarah's stock. The price they paid was not made public, but the newspapers estimated that it approached the half-million mark. Sarah sold the Kidder mansion as well and made plans to move to San Francisco. She officially tendered her resignation from the railroad on May 16, 1913.[25]

During Sarah's twelve years serving as president, she had managed to pay off $79,000 in funded debt, pay $182,122 interest on that debt, declare $116,256 in dividends on the stock, and add $179,877 to the undivided surplus. During her time in office, Sarah had mended roadbeds, put in new rails, purchased new rolling stock, and begun operating the line in an up-to-date manner.[26]

After toiling over the railroad, Sarah spent her time decorating her new home in Ingleside Terrace. According to the December 14, 1913, edition of the *San Francisco Examiner*, Sarah was described as a woman of means who was able to buy where conditions best suited her. "She spent months in southern California," the article read. "She said she was attracted by the beauties of Pasadena as a home community, but she concluded to wait until she had personally inspected the beautiful home sites in Oakland, Berkeley, Alameda, Marin County and those down the peninsula.[27]

"Mrs. Kidder frankly states that she had not thought of San Francisco as a city of homes until she spent a day in a touring car visiting and inspecting the restricted residence parks west of Twin Peaks. She spent one afternoon in Ingleside Terrace, saw the beautiful Pueblo home on the eminence at Paloma Avenue and Mercedes Way, and a few days later informed General Manager Joseph A. Leonard that she was ready to purchase it. She is having a garage built and is furnishing the home in keeping with its elegant interior finish, and will shortly appear in the directory of the exclusive residence park."[28]

In addition to personalizing her house, Sarah enjoyed traveling via automobile to various cities. She was fascinated with driving and would embark on long, cross-country excursions with friends.[29]

Sarah A. Kidder passed away on Friday, September 29, 1933. She had been suffering with ill health for several months before her death. She was laid to rest at the Cypress Lawn Memorial Park in Coloma, California. Sarah was ninety-one when she died.[30]

Twenty-nine years after Sarah retired as president of the Nevada County Narrow Gauge Railroad, the company petitioned the railroad commission to abandon the line. The old line, since its inception, had experienced countless ups and downs. Its bellowing engines had hauled ore and passengers in the days ahead of the truck and sedan, when the service was extremely important.[31]

CHAPTER 3

Helen Hunt Jackson:
The Poet's Railroad Tour

BETWEEN 1860 AND 1890, RAILROAD MILEAGE MULTIPLIED FROM 30,000 to 166,000. Within the first ten years after the Golden Spike ceremony joined the first transcontinental railway, three additional railroads spanned the land, and short lines had been united into systems linking innumerable tiny towns and villages to each other and to the great metropolitan cities.[1] Editorials and travel features extolling the advantage of train excursions appeared in newspapers and magazines across the country. Helen Hunt, a reporter for *Scribner's Monthly Magazine* and later *Century Magazine*, penned several stories about traveling across the frontier.[2]

The well-known, highly acclaimed poet and writer was born in Amherst, Massachusetts, in 1831. Helen was the daughter of Nathan Fiske, a professor of languages and religion at Amherst College. She was a strong-willed individual who cherished reading from an early age. She was the second-oldest child and experienced a great deal of tragedy growing up. Her two brothers died at infancy, and her mother, Deborah, struggled with tuberculosis. Shortly after her mother's death, Helen's father became a missionary to the Holy Land, and she and her sister were sent to live with relatives. In his absence, Nathan Fiske arranged for his daughters to attend select boarding schools. He died unexpectedly in 1847.[3]

In 1852, Helen married Captain Edward B. Hunt, a military engineer. In the second year of her marriage, she lost a child. Her husband was killed in 1863 by the explosion of a submarine gun of his own invention. Less than two years later, her second child, a son, died.[4]

Helen Hunt Jackson LIBRARY OF CONGRESS

Out of her loss and sorrow blossomed a great desire for writing. Helen's first poem, titled "Lifted Over" and about her son's passing, was published in 1865.[5] Her successful literary career began in 1866 when she moved to Newport, Massachusetts. In addition to poems, Helen wrote essays, children's stories, and travel pieces for magazines. Her first collection of writing published in book form was *Bits of Travel at Home*, written after she spent from 1868 to 1870 in Europe.[6]

In the spring of 1872, Helen and her friend, fellow author Susan Coolidge, traveled to California on the Union Pacific Railroad. Both women were to write helpful guides for ladies embarking on summer trips from the East Coast to the West Coast. The pair boarded the train in Chicago in mid-May. Helen's initial impressions of the vehicle that would be transporting them to points beyond the Mississippi were less than favorable.[7]

"Three nights and four days in the cars!" Helen recalled in her book *Bits of Travel at Home*. "These words haunted us and hindered our rest. What should we eat and drink, and wherewithal should we be clothed? No Scripture was strong enough to calm our anxious thoughts; no friend's experience of comfort and ease on the journey sounded credible enough to disarm our fears. 'Dust is dust,' said we, 'and railroad is railroad. All restaurant cooking in America is intolerable. We shall be wretched; nevertheless, we go.'[8]

"Our drawing-room? Yes, our drawing-room; and this is the plan of it: A small, square room, occupying the whole width of the car, excepting a narrow passageway on one side; four windows, two opening on this passageway and two opening out of doors; two doors, one opening into the car and one opening into a tiny closet, which held a washstand basin. This closet had another door, opening into another drawing-room beyond. No one but the occupants of the two drawing-rooms could have access to the bath-closet. On one side of our drawing-room a long sofa; on the other two large arm-chairs, which could be wheeled so as to face the sofa. Two shining spittoons and plenty of looking-glass, hooks high up on the sides, and silver-plated rods for curtains overhead, completed the list of furniture. Room on the floor for bags and bundles and baskets; room, too, for a third chair, and a third chair we had for a part of the way, an easy-chair, with a sloping back, which belonged to another of these luxurious Pullman cars."[9]

As the trip progressed, Helen lost herself in the scenery and the enormity of the frontier. "By hundreds of miles the rich prairie lands had unrolled themselves, smiled, and fled. On the very edges of the crumbling, dusty banks of our track stood pink, and blue, and yellow flowers, undisturbed. The homesteads in the distances looked like shining green fortresses, for nearly every house has a tree wall on two sides of it. The trees looked like poplars, but we could not be sure. Often we saw only the solid green square, the house being entirely concealed from view. As we drew near the Mississippi River, soft, low hills came into view on each side; tangled skeins of little rivers, shaded by tall trees, wound and unwound themselves side by side with us. A big bridge lay ready, on which we crossed; everybody standing on the platform of the cars, at their own risk, according to the explicit prohibition of the railroad company.[10]

" 'Make your beds now, ladies?' said the chamberman . . .

" 'Yes,' we replied. 'That is just what we most desire to see.'

"Presto! The seats of the arm-chairs pull out, and meet in the middle. The backs of the arm-chairs pull down, and lie flat on level with the seats. The sofa pulls out and opens into double width. The roof of our drawing-room opens and lets down, and makes two more bedsteads, which we, luckily, do not want; but from under their eaves come mattresses, pillows, sheets, pillow-cases, and curtains. The beds are made; the roof shut up again; the curtains hung across the glass part of the doors; the curtains drawn across the passage-way windows; the doors shut and locked; and we undress as entirely and safely as if we were in the best bedroom of a house not made with wheels. Because we are so comfortable, we lie awake a little, but not long; and that is the whole story of nights on the cars when the cars are built by Pullman and the sleeping is done in drawing-rooms.[11]

"Next morning, more prairie—unfenced now, undivided, unmeasured, unmarked, save by the different tints of different growths of grass or grain; great droves of cattle grazing here and there; acres of willow saplings, pale yellowish green; and solitary trees, which look like hermits in a wilderness. These, and now then a shapeless village, which looks even lonelier than the empty loneliness by which it is surrounded—these are all for hours and hours. We think, 'now we are getting out into the great spaces. This is what the word "West" has sounded like.'"[12]

Helen was transfixed by the vast open space that stretched out on either side of the Platte River in Nebraska. She contemplated the brave men and women who had made the journey across the plains by wagon

PULLMAN'S PALACE DINING CAR.

The Pullman's Palace Car, where author Helen Hunt Jackson and other passengers enjoyed their meals AUTHOR'S COLLECTION

train and imagined traveling past the graves of emigrants who perished along the way. She marveled at the grand sunsets, the wildlife that dotted the route, and the hamlets where the train stopped.[13]

"Early one morning, we saw antelopes," Helen later wrote. "They were a great way off, and, while they stood still, might as well have been big goats or small cows; but, when they were good enough to bound, no eye could mistake them. The sight of these consoled us for having passed through the buffalo country in the night. It also explained the nature of the steaks we had been eating. How should steaks be tender cut out of that acrobatic sort of muscle? We passed also the outposts of Prairie Dog Town. The owls and rattlesnakes were 'not receiving,' apparently; but the droll, little squirrel-like puppies met us most cordially. The mixture of defiance and terror, of attack and retreat, in their behavior was as funny as it always is in small dogs, who bark and run, in other places. But the number and manner of shelters made it unspeakably droll here. I am not sure that I actually saw the whole of any one prairie dog at a time. What I chiefly saw were ends of tails going into holes, and tips of noses sticking out to bark.[14]

"We were invited to dine at Cheyenne. 'Cheyenne City,' it is called. Most of the buildings which we saw were one-story wooden ones, small, square, with no appearance of roofs, only a square, sharp-cornered front, like a section of board fence. These all faced the railroad station, were painted with conspicuous signs, such as 'Billiard Saloon,' 'Sample Room,' 'Meals for Fifty Cents;' and, in the doors of most of them, as the train arrived, there stood a woman or a boy, ringing a shrill bell furiously. It is curious, at these stations, to see how instantly the crowd of passengers assorts itself, and divides into grades, of people seeking for the best; people seeking for the cheapest; and other people, most economical of all, who buy only hot drinks, having brought a grocery store and a restaurant along with them in a basket-tower."[15]

From Cheyenne, Helen and her friend, Susan, proceeded to Sherman, Wyoming, while riding in the engine. The train required two engines to get over the steep mountain pass. "The throbbing puffs, almost under our feet, sounded like the quick-drawn, panting breaths of some giant creature," Helen recalled about the venture. "Once in every three or four

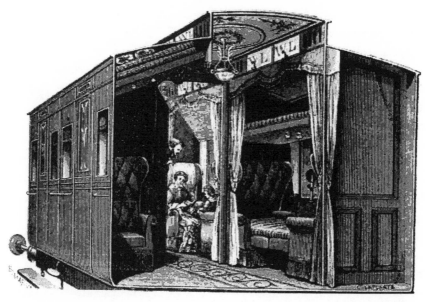

A look inside the drawing room Helen Hunt Jackson described in her book *Bits of Travel at Home* AUTHOR'S COLLECTION

minutes, the great breastplate door opened; and we looked into its heart of fire, and fed it with fuel. Once in every three or four minutes, one of the keepers crept along on its sides, out to its very mount, and poured oil into every joint: he strode its neck, and anointed every valve. His hand seemed to pat it lovingly, as he came back, holding on by the shining rods and knobs and handles. I almost forgot to look at the stretches of snow, the forests of pines, the plateaus of mountain-tops, on either hand, so absorbed was I in the sense of supernatural motion."[16]

On the morning of the fourth day of Helen's journey, the Union Pacific train arrived in Utah. Both Helen and Susan were moved by the wondrous surroundings. "We looked out on a desert of sage-brush and sand; but the desert had infinite beauties of shape, and the sage had pathos of color," Helen noted in her memoir. "Why has the sage-brush been so despised, so held up to the scorn of men? It is simply a miniature olive tree. In tint, in shape, the resemblance is wonderful. Travelers never tire of recording the sad and subtle beauty of Mediterranean slopes, gray with the soft, thick, rounded tops of olive orchards. The stretches of these sage-grown plains have the same tints, the same roundings and blendings of soft, thick foliage; the low sand-hills have endless variety of outline, and all strangely suggestive. There are fortresses, palisades, roof slopes with dormer windows, hollows like cradles, and here and there vivid green oases. In these oases cattle graze.... Then comes a tract of stony country, where the rocks seem also as significant and suggestive as the sand-hills—castles, and pillars, and altars, and spires: it is impossible to believe that human hands have not wrought them."[17]

Helen and Susan enjoyed watching the amazing sights from the observation car. The experience left Helen convinced that no train should be without such an open car. She was particularly appreciative of the car when the vehicle reached Utah's Echo Canyon.[18]

"Rocks of red and pale yellow color were piled and strewn on either hand in a confusion so wild that it was majestic," Helen later recalled, "many of them looked like gateways and walls and battlements of fortifications; many of them seemed poised on points, just ready to fall; others rose massive and solid, from terraces which stretched away beyond our sight. The railroad track is laid (is hung would seem a truer phrase) high up on the right-hand wall of the [canyon], that is, on the wall of stone. The old emigrant road ran at the base of the opposite wall (the wall of grassy slopes), close on the edge of the river. Just after we entered the [canyon], as we looked down to the river, we saw an emigrant party in sore trouble on that road. The river was high and overflowed the road; the crumbling, gravelly precipice rose up hundreds of feet sheer from the water; the cattle which the poor man was driving were trying to run up the precipice, but all to no purpose; the wife and children sat on logs by the wagon, apathetically waiting, nothing to be done but to wait there in that wild and desolate spot till the river chose to give them right of way again.[19]

"They were so many hundred feet below us that the cattle seemed calves and the people tiny puppets, as we looked over the narrow rim of earth and stone which upheld us in the air. But I envied them. They would see the [canyon], know it. To us it would be only a swift and vanishing dream. Even while we are whirling through, it grows unreal. Flowers of blue, yellow, purple are flying past, seemingly almost under our wheels. We look over them down into broader spaces, where there are homesteads and green meadows. Then the [canyon] walls close in again, and, looking down we see only a silver thread of river; looking up, we see only a blue belt of sky."[20]

From Echo Canyon, the friends traveled to Weber Canyon.

"The [glorious canyon] opens suddenly into a broad, beautiful meadow, in which the river seems to rest rather than to run," Helen explained. "A line of low houses, a Mormon settlement, marks the banks; fields of grain and grass glitter in the early green; great patches of blue lupine on every hand look blue as blue water at a distance, the flowers are set so thick. Only a few moments of this, however, and we are again in a rocky gorge, where there is barely room for the river, and no room for us, except on a bridge. This, too, is named for that same popular person, 'Devil's Gate.' The river foams and roars under our feet as we go through. Now comes another open plain, wide, sunny, walled about by snow mountains, and holding a town. This is Ogden, and the shining water which lies in sight to the left is the Great Salt Lake!"[21]

The Union Pacific Railroad ended in Ogden, Utah, where the Central Pacific Railroad began. A change in railroads also meant a change in railroad cars. Helen's luggage was transferred, but she didn't immediately proceed with the trip. Helen and her friend's accommodations would no longer be on a Pullman drawing-room car but on a Silver Palace Car. "We are told that there are good reasons why no mortal can engage a section of a sleeping-car to be ready for him at Ogden on any particular day," Helen later wrote. "Through passengers must be accommodated first. Through passengers, no doubt, see the justice of this. Way passengers cannot be expected to. But we do most emphatically realize the bearing of it when we arrive at Ogden from Salt Lake City at four o'clock in the afternoon, and find anxious men standing patiently in line, forty deep, before the ticket-office, biding their chance of having to sit up for the two nights which must be spent on the road between Ogden and San Francisco. It was a desperate hour for that ticket agent; and the crowd was a study for an artist. Most to be pitied of all were the married men, whose nervous wives kept plucking them by the coattails and drawing them out of the line once in five minutes, to propose utterly impracticable devices for circumventing or hurrying the ticket-agent.[22]

33

"I do not know how many, if any, of the forty unfortunates rode all the way bedless to San Francisco; for our first anxiety as to whether we should each get a section was soon merged in our second, which was almost as great, what we should do with ourselves in it."[23]

Helen had a fine appreciation for the landscape she witnessed during her cross-country tour, but at times found the mode of transportation lacking.[24]

"A latent sense of justice restrains me from attempting to describe a section," Helen noted. "It is impossible to be just to a person or a thing disliked. I dislike the sleeping-car sections more than I ever have disliked, ever shall dislike, or ever can dislike anything in the world. Therefore, I will not describe one. I will speak only of the process of going to bed and getting up in it.[25]

"Fancy a mattress laid on the bottom shelf in your cupboard, and the cupboard door shut. You have previously made choice among your possessions which ones you will have put underneath your shelf, where you cannot get at them, and which ones you must have, and will therefore keep all night on the foot of your bed. Accurate memory and judicious selection, under such circumstances, are impossible. No sooner is the cupboard door shut than you remember that several indispensable articles are under the shelf. But the door is locked, and you can't get out. By which I mean that the porter has put up the curtain in front of your section, and of the opposite section, and you have partially undressed, and can't step out into the narrow aisle without encountering the English gentleman, who is going by to heat water on the stove at the end of the car; and, even if you didn't encounter him, you can't get at the things which have been stowed away under your shelf, unless you lie down at full length on the floor to reach them; and you can't lie down at full length on the floor, because most of the floor is under your opposite neighbor's shelf. So I said the door was locked simply to express the hopelessness of the situation.[26]

"Then you sit cross-legged on your bed; because, of course, you can't sit on the edge of the shelf after the cupboard door is shut—that is, the curtain is put up so close to the edge of your bed that, if you do sit there in the natural human manner, your knees and feet will be in the way of the English gentleman when he passes. Sitting cross-legged on your bed, you take off a few of your clothes, if you have courage; and then you cast about to think what you shall do with them. It is quite light in the cupboard, for there is a little kerosene lamp in a tiny glass-doored niche in the wall; and it gives light enough to show you that there isn't a hook or an edge of anything on which a single article can be hung."[27]

The first night Helen and her friend, Susan, traveled on the Central Pacific Railroad, they passed over the Great American Desert. All they could see upon waking the next morning was sand and sagebrush.[28]

"The tints are exquisite," Helen remembered. "We shall not be weary of it if it lasts all day. And it did last all day. All day long tints of gray and brown; sometimes rocky ravines, with low, dark growths on their sides; sometimes valleys, which the guide book said were fertile, but which to us looked just as gray and brown as the plains."[29]

The next stop for Helen and her companion was Humboldt Station in northern California. The pair had been looking forward to reaching the station because it meant supper, but, when they stopped, thoughts of supper fled.

"Four thousand feet above the sea, among alkali sands and stony volcanic beds, there stood a brilliant green oasis," Helen recalled. "Clover fields, young trees, and vegetable gardens surrounded the little house. In front was a fountain, which sparkled in the sun. Around it was a broad rim of grass and white clover. An iron railing enclosed it. It was a pathetic sight to see rough men, even men from the emigrant car, stretching their hands through the railing to pick a blade of grass or a clover blossom.[30]

"One great, burly fellow lifted up his little girl, and, swinging her over the iron spikes, set her down in the grass saying, 'There! I'd like to see ye steppin' on green grass once more.' It was a test of loyalty to green fields and there were no traitors. We had not dreamed that we had grown so hungry for sight of true summer. Just as the train was about to start, I remembered a gentle-faced woman in our car who had not come out. I reached into the grassy rim, without looking, and picked a clover leaf to carry her as a token. I gave it to her, without having looked closely at it. 'And a four leafed clover, too!' she exclaimed, as she took it."[31]

Although Helen found the Salt Lake desert beautiful, she was excited about the change of scenery California had to offer. "We awoke in the

Sierras," Helen noted. "As far as we could see on either hand rose snowy tops of mountains. We were on them, below them, among them, all at once. Some were covered with pines and firs; some were glistening and bare. We looked down into ravines and gorges which were so deep they were black. Tops of firs, which we knew must be hundreds of feet high, seemed to make only a solid mossy bed below us. The sun shone brilliantly on the crests and upper slopes; now and then a sharp gleam of light showed a lake or a river far down among the dark and icy walls. It seemed almost as if these lights came from our train, as if we bore a gigantic lantern, which flashed its light in and out as we went winding and leaping from depth to depth, from peak to peak.[32]

"I think nothing could happen in life which could make any human being who had looked out on this scene forget it. Presently we entered the snow-sheds. These were dreary, but could not wholly interrupt the grandeur. Fancy miles upon miles of covered bridge, with black and grimy snow-drifts, or else still blacker and grimier gutters of water, on each side the track (for the snow-sheds keep out only part of the snow); through the seams between the boards, sometimes through open spaces where boards have fallen, whirling glimpses of snow-drifts outside, of tops of trees, of tops of mountains, of bottoms of canyons—this is snow-shed traveling. And there are thirty-nine miles of it on the Central Pacific Railroad. It was like being borne along half blindfolded through the upper air. I felt as if I knew how the Sierras might look to eagles flying over in haste, with their eyes fixed on the sun.[33]

" 'Breakfast in a snow-shed this morning, ladies,' said Frank, our chambermaid. True; the snow-shed branched off like a mining gallery, widened, and took in the front of a little house, whose door was set wide open, and whose breakfast-bell was ringing as we jumped out of the cars. We walked up to the dining room over icy rock. Through openings at each side, where the shed joined the house, we looked out upon fields of snow, and firs, and rocky peaks; but the sun shone like the sun of June and we had not a sensation of chill."[34]

After breakfast in a snowshed, Helen and Susan focused all their attention on the view as the train descended from its high position in the Sierras. "In a few miles we had gone down three thousand feet, the brakes all the while holding us back, lest we should roll too fast," Helen noted about the ride out of the mountains. "Flowers sprang up into sight, as if conjured by a miracle out of the ice; green spaces, too, and little branches, with trees and shrubs around them. The great American Canyon seemed to open its arms, finding us bold enough to enter. Its walls are two thousand feet high, and are rifted by other canyons running down, each with its tiny silver thread of water, till they are lost in the abysses of fir-trees below.[35]

"The mining villages looked gay as gardens. Every shanty had vines and shrubs and flowers about it. On all the hillsides were long, narrow wooden troughs, full of running water, like miniature canals, but swift, like brooks. One fancied that the water had a golden gleam in it, left from the precious gold it had washed. Still down, down, out of the snow into bloom, out of winter into spring, so suddenly that the winter and the spring seemed equally unreal, and we half looked for summer's grain and autumn's vintage, station by station. Nothing could have seemed too soon, too startling. We doubled Cape Horn, in the sunny weather, as gaily as if we had been on a light-boat's deck; but we were sitting, standing, clinging on the steps and platforms of a heavy railroad train, whose track bent at a sharp angle around a rocky wall which rose up hundreds of feet straight in the air, and reached down hundreds of feet into the green valley beneath."[36]

It was noon in late June when Helen Hunt and Susan Coolidge reached Colfax, California.

"According to all calendars, there had been months between our breakfast and our dinner," Helen recalled. "Men and boys ran up and down in the cars, offering us baskets of ripe strawberries and huge bunches of red, white, and pink roses. Gay placards advertising circuses and concerts were on the walls and fences of Colfax. Yellow stages stood ready to carry people over smooth, red roads, which were to be seen winding off in many ways. 'Grass Valley,' 'You Bet,' and 'Little York' were three of the names."[37]

Executives with the Union and Central Pacific Railroads hoped articles written by Helen's overland trip would entice women to come West via the rails, which had made regular tourism to California possible. They desired the same outcome from the essay written by Helen's traveling companion, Susan Coolidge. Susan's report titled "A Few Hints on the California Journey" appeared in the May 1873 edition of *Scribner's Monthly Magazine*.[38]

A year after Helen's article about her railroad journey appeared in *Scribner's Monthly Magazine*, the writer moved from the Baltimore area to Colorado. She was suffering with a bronchial condition, and doctors believed she could find relief in the high elevation. Helen was also struggling with depression. She'd never been able to recover from the death of her husband and children. The hope was that Helen could have her physical and emotional health restored in the growing community of Colorado Springs.[39]

She moved into the Colorado Springs Hotel. Her fellow boarders were pleasant, particularly a Pennsylvania Quaker by the name of William Sharpless Jackson. William was a banker and owner of the Denver and Rio Grande Railroad. Together they took long drives into the mountains. Daily, the excursions grew longer. They traveled to Fairplay, Central City, and Denver.[40]

On October 22, 1875, Helen Hunt married William Jackson in a Quaker ceremony in New Hampshire. The couple traveled a great deal on the Denver and Rio Grande Railroad. Helen continually submitted articles to eastern magazines about her exploration of Colorado while on the train.[41]

CHAPTER 4

Laura Bullion:
The Wild Bunch Train Robber

The Great Northern Railway Coast Flyer No. 3 pulled away from the train depot in Malta, Montana, at 11:45 p.m. on July 3, 1901. Malta was a typical cow town with a broad, rutted lane of brown dust running between a double row of false-fronted, framed buildings. Horses, their tails swishing idly at buzzing flies, stood hipshot at the hitchracks that lined the front of every store. The Flyer was headed west to Wagner, Montana, a slightly bigger cow town that greatly resembled Malta right down to the flies.[1]

Among the passengers traveling to Wagner was train robber Ben "Blackie" Kilpatrick. Kilpatrick was a member of outlaw Butch Cassidy's Wild Bunch. Two additional Wild Bunch gang members were making the trip with Kilpatrick: Harvey "Kid Curry" Logan and O. C. Hanks. Thomas Jones, the train's engineer, brought the vehicle to a sudden halt less than six miles east of Wagner. Logan had a revolver leveled at Jones's head, encouraging him to stop the train. The gunman had snuck aboard the tender car* and onto the engine cab. The Flyer's fireman,** Mike O'Neill, was with the engineer when he was overtaken, and neither man dared move with a gun pointed at them.[2]

---

* A tender or coal car is a special rail vehicle hauled by a steam locomotive containing its fuel (wood, coal, or oil) and water.

** According to CareerMatch.com., "the term 'Railroad Fireman' referred to the train crewman who shoveled coal into the furnace and tended the boiler on an old-fashioned steam locomotive. . . . In this role, you're still responsible for the fuel needs of the train, and maintaining the locomotive and related railroad facilities."

Logan motioned for O'Neill to disembark the train and uncouple the baggage and express cars from the passenger cars. He reluctantly complied. While the engineer was following orders, a rancher named John Cunningham noticed the peculiar display and spurred his horse toward the scene for a better look. Recognizing the train was being robbed, he jerked his roan in the direction of Malta, and the animal started to run. Kilpatrick, who had jumped off the passenger car, shot at the rancher, knocking his horse out from under him. John Cunningham quickly picked himself up and began running in the direction of the cow town. A few curious onlookers dared to lean their heads out the windows of the car to witness the action. Kilpatrick fired at them and warned them to remain in their seats. No one evinced a desire to disobey the order. A brakeman named Woodside and a traveling auditor refused to comply with the outlaw's orders, and both were shot through the shoulder.[3]

The three bandits made their way to the express car and demanded the mail clerk and express messenger guarding the cargo inside to step away from the safe.[4]

According to the July 4, 1901, edition of the *Great Falls Tribune*, the robbers then "proceeded to blow open the large safe and secured a booty estimated at $50,000." The man with the dynamite was identified as Ben Kilpatrick. The article noted that a fourth bandit was waiting near the location where the train came to rest. That individual, dressed in trousers, work shirt, boots, and duster had possession of the explosives used in the crime and provided the horses the outlaws used to escape.[5]

Several months after the holdup occurred, law enforcement agents discovered the fourth accomplice was actually a woman disguised as a man. Laura Bullion, a twenty-five-year-old prostitute from Texas, was Kilpatrick's lover and coconspirator.[6]

By ten o'clock in the evening of the train robbery, a posse had been dispatched from Malta to track down the bandits and arrest them. Law enforcement believed the gang was traveling southwest through the Missouri Breaks.[7]

Several days after the robbery, an auditor for the Great Northern Express Railway informed authorities the exact amount of the loss by the holdup was $41,500. All but $300 was currency sent from Washington to

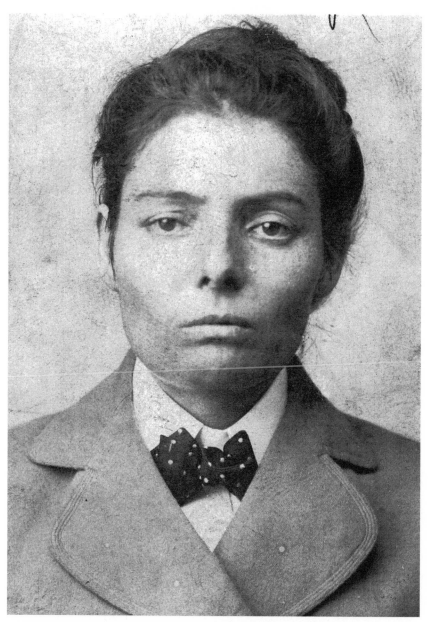

Laura Bullion, the famous woman train robber

the Montana National Bank of Helena. The remaining money belonged to Great Northern Railway. The consignment to the Montana bank consisted of bank notes printed in sheets of $10 and $20 bills. Only nine were signed by the president and cashier of the bank, but all could be readily passed without their signatures.[8] Executives at Great Northern Railway were informed of the identity of the men who robbed the express safe on July 10, 1901.[9]

Pinkerton detectives sent from the St. Paul, Minnesota, office were instrumental in determining the guilty parties. A spokesman for the railroad declined to give the names of the suspects to the press. They preferred to wait until the Pinkertons had made an arrest. "If the Pinkertons are correct, the men are experienced hands and have held up trains on other roads," a Great Northern Railway spokesperson told reporters.[10]

Officials at Great Northern Railway might not have wanted to divulge the culprits' names, but the sheriff of Ramsey County, Minnesota, had no trouble sharing the identity of the train robbers and news of the $5,500 reward offered by the railroad for their capture. "The robbers are described as being George Parker, alias George Cassidy, alias 'Butch' Cassidy, alias Ingerfield; Harvey Logan, alias Harvey Curry, alias 'Kid' Curry, alias Bob Jones, alias Tom Jones; and Harry Longabaugh, alias Harry Alonzo," the sheriff is quoted as saying in the July 27, 1901, edition of the *Saint Paul Globe*.[11]

"The circular provided to all law enforcement agencies gives in brief what is known of the criminal records of the three men, from which it appears that Cassidy is known in the states of Wyoming, Utah, Idaho, Colorado, and Nevada, and that he has served terms in Wyoming for grand larceny.[12]

"Logan is the one who murdered a man named Pike at Landusky, Montana, on December 25, 1894, and is a fugitive from justice. He has since been implicated in a number of crimes, among them the robbery of a Union Pacific train at Wilcox, Wyoming.[13]

"Longabaugh has a long criminal record, and has, since he was a boy, been repeatedly arrested for horse stealing, robberies, and other crimes. In 1892 he held up a Great Northern train with some other men near Malta, Montana, and although two of his confederates were apprehended and

Drawing of the robbery of the Great Northern Railway Coast Flyer No. 3
AUTHOR'S COLLECTION

given long terms, he escaped, and has since been implicated in the robbery of a number of banks at Winnemucca, Nevada, and Belle Fourche, South Dakota. For the last crime he was arrested, but escaped from jail at Deadwood on October 31, 1897.[14]

"The circular issued by Great Northern Railway states that included in the spoils of the Wagner raid was a package of $10,000 of incomplete currency lacking the signature of the president and cashier of the National Bank of Helena, Montana. The package consisted of 800 sheets, with four notes on each being three $10 and one $20 bills. They also took a similar package containing $500 intended for the American National Bank of Helena."[15]

The authorities were only partially right about who robbed the Great Northern Railway Flyer No. 3. Butch Cassidy and the Sundance Kid were nowhere around when the crime was perpetrated, and no one suspected a woman had a hand in the theft.[16]

The Pinkerton files from the early 1900s list Laura Bullion as a "consort of criminals." She was born in Mertzon, Texas, on October 4, 1876, to parents with questionable morals. Her father, Ed, was a thief who tried his hand at robbing a train in December 1897, and her mother, Fereby Elizabeth Bullion, was a strumpet who preferred the company of a variety of bad men over her husband. Laura and her siblings were primarily raised by her mother's parents, Elliot and Serena Byler, in Knickerbocker, Texas. The area of the Southwest where the teenage Laura was living was a hub of outlawry. The Bylers tried unsuccessfully to steer their granddaughter away from such an influence.[17]

Among the men of questionable character in and around Knickerbocker with whom Laura associated were Tom "Black Jack" Ketchum and his brother, Sam; Ben Kilpatrick; his brother, George; and William "News" Carver, the latter of which was married to Laura's aunt, Viana E. Blyer. When Laura left her family's home, she headed to San Antonio. She took a job at a brothel owned and operated by Fannie Porter, and, using the name Della Rose, the young woman began entertaining clients.[18]

Porter's bordello was a favorite location of Butch Cassidy and the Sundance Kid, alias Robert Leroy Parker and Harry Longabaugh. The two leaders of the outlaw gang known as the Wild Bunch spent time with several of the women in Fannie's employ. Ben Kilpatrick and William Carver, who joined the Wild Bunch in the late 1890s, were among those who frequented the establishment with Butch and Sundance. Will Carver took up with Laura. Viana had died shortly after she and Will married, and Laura's similarities to her mother's sister attracted the grieving widower.[19]

The soiled doves and the outlaws socialized outside the brothel. Laura and the other girls who worked in the house proved themselves to be trustworthy with the identity of the men who visited them. They could keep a secret. Laura's ability to keep a confidence was one of the qualities Ben Kilpatrick found appealing. When Will's attention turned to another woman at Fannie's, Ben seized the opportunity to be with Laura.[20] She accompanied him to the Wild Bunch hideout, Hole-in-the-Wall, in northern Wyoming. Just how many robberies Laura assisted Kilpatrick with is not known. The only certainty is that she was an accomplice in the Great Northern Railway robbery near Wagner, Montana.[21]

Between July 1901, when the train was held up, and early November 1901, several posses were formed to track the train robbers. Law enforcement agents from Chouteau County, Montana, were so certain they would capture the outlaws they brought along a coroner and a handful of caskets.[22]

In early November 1901, stolen banknotes from the Wagner robbery began turning up in St. Louis, Missouri. Police in the city, along with the Pinkerton Detective Agency, managed to track the passing of the notes to Ben Kilpatrick. He had been residing at a hotel near the waterfront. He was taken into custody on November 5, 1901, and was uncooperative with authorities. He refused to identify himself or answer any questions. While searching through his personal belongings, authorities found a key to a room at the Laclede Hotel. The following morning when the police were able to search the premises, they met Laura Bullion leaving the hotel room with a suitcase full of the forged banknotes. She was arrested on the spot.[23]

Like Kilpatrick, Laura refused to answer authorities' queries. According to the November 8, 1901, edition of the *St. Louis Republic*, law enforcement agents noted, "It was like questioning the Sphinx." Superintendent Schumacher of the Pinkerton Detective Agency tried to get Laura to cooperate, but she merely yawned and pretended to fall asleep. "The prisoner exuded silence and noninformation at every pore," the *St. Louis Republic* article read, "and the amount of knowledge of her antecedents they did not acquire would fill so many volumes it would bankrupt Carnegie to house them. She said less in more time than a Republican campaign orator. She was impervious to the volley of questions hurled at her as a Republican organ to the truth about the state finances. Chief William Desmond, chief of detectives in St. Louis, was disappointed, but not disheartened, laid her away at midnight like an uncut volume of Browning."[24]

With neither Laura nor Kilpatrick willing to talk about the robbery or cooperate with authorities and give them the names of all those involved in the Wagner train holdup, detectives with the St. Louis Police Department decided to fill in the blanks themselves. Chief Desmond requested the wanted circular issued by the Pinkerton Detective Agency that included a description of the bandits. Given the description, the St. Louis police said it was determined that Kilpatrick was indeed Harry Longabaugh. After St. Louis detectives examined Laura's belongings, they were convinced they had apprehended the notorious Sundance Kid. Among her personal effects was a notebook in which she had written "Harry Longbaugh [*sic*] black hair, steel grey eyes, very fair skin when not tanned by the sun." The man in custody resembled the description Laura gave. For the authorities, that was another confirmation they had one of the leaders of the Wild Bunch behind bars.[25]

Laura knew the Sundance Kid wasn't in jail, but she continued with the charade when the police asked her about the journal on November 14, 1901. "I have known the prisoner who is called Longbaugh [*sic*], since the latter part of April," Laura told detectives. "It was in Fort Worth, Texas, that I first met him. Since that time, we have lived in various cities and have gone under different names in every place that we visited. He had plenty of money, and I never asked him any questions as to where he got it. He gave me the money that was in his possession when I was arrested. I don't know where he got it. I don't know anything about that Wagner robbery."[26]

Laura admitted to forging the name of the cashier of the National Bank of Helena on the notes found in her possession. She also admitted that the names she and her partner had registered under at the hotel were false. The couple had registered as J. W. Rose and wife of Vicksburg, Mississippi. Laura went on to tell authorities that when she met the man they thought was the Sundance Kid, he introduced himself to her as Cunningham. It wasn't until she found a pocket dictionary in his coat with the name Harry Longabaugh written in the front page that she knew his true name. According to the November 15, 1902, edition of the *San Angelo Press*, Laura told Chief Desmond that when Cunningham gave her seven thousand dollars in unsigned Helena National Bank notes, she was convinced that he was Longabaugh the train robber. She said she never mentioned her suspicions to Cunningham.[27]

A picture of the man St. Louis police believed was Longabaugh was circulated to various sheriff offices in the Southwest shortly after the initial arrests in the Wagner robbery were made. In mid-November 1901, a telegram was sent to Chief Desmond in St. Louis from Sheriff House in Concho, Texas, identifying the man in the picture as Ben Kilpatrick.

Known by Sheriff House as the "Lone Texan," Kilpatrick was wanted for killing a man.[28]

"You are wanted for murder down there," the chief reportedly asked the accused. "Now, who did you kill?"

"I don't remember having any trouble down there," replied the prisoner. Then he stopped talking.[29]

"The police were then convinced that the suspect was Ben Kilpatrick of Paintrock, Texas," the November 16, 1901, edition of the *Saint Paul Globe* noted. "A letter containing an authentic picture of Kilpatrick was received this afternoon from Sheriff House. The likeness between the picture and the prisoner is unmistakable. When the photograph was shown to the prisoner, he was visibly agitated. He compressed his lips but did not say anything.[30]

"Within ten minutes after the photograph was shown, a telegram was received, this one from R. B. Kirk, the sheriff of Billinger County, Texas, saying that the picture of the supposed Longabaugh had been positively identified there as that of Ben Kilpatrick."[31]

Laura Bullion became somewhat of a legend while waiting to be tried for her part in the Wagner train robbery. She was referred to in some newspapers as "astonishing" and "staggering." She claimed she robbed trains for the "sheer pleasure of it" and because "she was a devoted wife helping her husband loot." An article in the December 12, 1901, edition of the *Anaconda Standard* called her "a remarkable woman criminal."[32]

"When the police of this city arrested Laura Bullion, or, as she is better known, Mrs. Della Rose, they captured one of the most remarkable woman criminals of whom there is any record," the *Anaconda Standard* article read. "Mrs. Rose, as far as is known, is the only woman who ever assisted in a train robbery in this country. Dressed in man's attire, she helped her husband in the hold-up of a Great Northern train in Montana a few weeks ago and the theft of $85,000 in new and unsigned bank notes from the safe of the express car. The woman's husband, Harry Longabaugh, alias J. W. Rose, also has a record as a daring and desperate criminal.[33]

"Longabaugh, or Rose, and Mrs. Rose were arrested on the same day. A reward of $6,500 had been offered for the arrest of any of the persons concerned in the robbery. It was not until after Mrs. Rose had been arrested that she was suspected of having taken part in the great train robbery. But certain admissions which she let slip at the time of her arrest aroused suspicion and a remarkable chain of circumstantial evidence is now being linked together against her. The robbery of the Great Northern express occurred three miles east of Wagner Station, Montana. It was the work of three persons."[34]

The *Anaconda Standard* article contained several errors, not the least of which was the true identity of Laura's cohort in crime. An article in the December 8, 1901, edition of the *Inter Ocean* also contained a few inaccuracies. The report maintained that Laura was the lead gunman at the train robbery. "She was wearing a mask, but appeared to be in authority, was very energetic, and utterly reckless in life. She discharged bullets like a Mexican gun." Laura took part in the crime but never fired a weapon. The truth obviously wasn't considered as exciting as the sensational version many newspapers decided to print.[35]

Laura Bullion and Ben Kilpatrick's trials were held in early December 1901. Ben was found guilty and sentenced to fifteen years in prison in the state penitentiary at Jefferson City, Missouri. Laura was also found guilty and sentenced to five years at the Massachusetts Correctional Institution for Women.[36]

The public's fascination with the only woman to belong to the Wild Bunch continued long after Laura was incarcerated. The robberies in which she allegedly participated grew from one to six while she was living out her sentence. Readers were intrigued with a female train robber. "It's hard for most to comprehend," a story in the June 12, 1904, edition of the *St. Louis Post-Dispatch* noted. "A woman dressed in men's attire who assisted in the hard riding raids perpetrated by the outlaw gang from Wyoming."[37]

Since the train robbery in the summer of 1901, officials at Great Northern Railway had taken steps to prevent such a crime from occurring on future passages. In addition to adding more security onboard the vehicles, the rail line decided to add a posse car to the train. The car was able to accommodate several horses and law enforcement agents that could be dispatched at a moment's notice. Other railroad lines such as the Union Pacific had already employed such measures for tracking gangs like the Wild Bunch in 1900. Great Northern Railway had been slow to add a posse car, and that's the reason they were a target for the outlaws.[38]

Laura's affection for and devotion to Ben Kilpatrick only strengthened during her time behind bars. The two regularly corresponded, and she even became friends with Ben's mother. The two exchanged letters, and Mrs. Kilpatrick encouraged Laura to stay strong and focus on the future. In an interview with the *St. Louis Post-Gazette* in mid-September 1905, Laura shared what life had been like since she had been sentenced.[39]

"Prison life is what the prisoners make it," she told the newspaper reporter. "The officials do their best. The matron is kind, but prisoners are like so many children. They play the games of children, and to them each day is for itself. They forget things easily. It is no place for a young woman. There are some girls there, and it is hard to think of what they have learned.[40]

"Women prisoners do not wear ugly uniforms as do the men. Our dresses were made of checked goods and cut after a fashion that was probably the style when grandmother was a girl—the skirt plain and sewed to the waist, which is buttoned down the front. The skirt fastens at the side. Some of the women who sew try to make their dresses look well but the garb is well known in the city.[41]

"The only hard work is contract work—the making of overalls and shirts. As I was a federal prisoner, they could not make me do that. The women who were there for other offenses must do contract work. I like to do drawn work, that helps pass time. Some of the women do beautiful fancy work.[42]

"We were permitted to write letters every Sunday and, when necessary, to write specials through the week. We received plenty of food, and it was usually good, but there was little variety."[43]

Laura explained that she didn't talk much in prison and when she did speak, she chose her words carefully. "I saved myself many difficulties by not talking much and carrying no tales," she noted. "I was ignorant of a great many things when I went to prison. I know too much now. I knew the prairies then. I had traveled across Arizona and New Mexico, but I didn't know the wickedness of the cities."[44]

Laura didn't want anyone to get the impression she blamed Ben or her family for her downfall. "They tried to get me to say things in court about Ben, but I wouldn't," she explained. "What good is a person if she can't keep to herself that which she is told? Besides, I wouldn't tell on him. I'd rather be sentenced. I trusted in people before I went to the penitentiary. I don't now. That's what it has cost me. A woman can influence a man much. It was my fault that we came to St. Louis. I wanted to come; we came, and trouble resulted, but Ben never blamed me."[45]

Laura was released from prison in September 1905 and shortly thereafter traveled to St. Louis to meet with Assistant District Attorney Horace L. Dyer to plead for a reduction in sentence for Ben Kilpatrick. The attorney informed her she needed to petition President Roosevelt. He explained that her petition would then be turned over to the pardon attorney, and it would be returned to St. Louis for the approval of the US District Attorney.[46]

Laura thanked Assistant District Attorney Dyer for meeting with her and promised to follow the procedure he laid out for her. She informed Dyer that once she had completed the steps he suggested, she would go to Atlanta, where Kilpatrick had been moved and was being held, and wait to hear from the government about her request. She rented a room at a boardinghouse opposite the penitentiary under the name of Frieda Arnold.[47]

Ben Kilpatrick was released from prison on June 13, 1911, having served one-third of his sentence. The moment he left the gates of the Atlanta facility, he was greeted by Texas authorities who escorted him to Concho County to stand trial on a murder charge from 1897. Laura followed Ben, determined to stand by him until the matter could be settled. The case against Kilpatrick was dismissed due to lack of evidence.[48]

On March 12, 1912, Ben Kilpatrick and another outlaw named E. Welch attempted to hold up the Southern Pacific train near Sanderson, Texas. Express messenger David Trousdale stopped the two train robbers before they could successfully complete the job. The train made an unscheduled stop at a bridge near the town of Eldridge. A fire had been built near the tracks where it was later believed a third bandit was waiting with horses so the trio could ride into the hills after the money had been stolen.[49]

"The first we knew of the trouble was when the engineer knocked on the right hand door of our car, and we were ordered to get out and go up to the engine," a second express messenger named J. K. Regan who was on the train explained in an article in the March 14, 1912, edition of the *El Paso Herald*. "We were covered with rifles by the two men, who had their heads covered with black cloths, and who made us climb on the engine while one of them poked his gun in the porter's nose and made him uncouple the baggage car, mail car and engine from the remainder of the train.[50]

"We then ran about two miles west with the men covering the engineer to make him stop. When we stopped, one of the men made us go into the mail car and slit the sacks of mail so that they could get the valuable packages out. The man told us that he was going to make us help him get the stuff across the Mexican line. He made one of the mail clerks assist in opening the mail, although none of it was carried out of the car.[51]

"From the mail car he made us go into our own car. Like a fool, he walked in front of us and Trousdale was ahead of me. There was a wooden mallet in the corner of the car to the right of the end door through which we entered. It was used to break up ice for icing oysters in transit. Trousdale saw it and while the man had his back to him, he cracked him one with it over the head and proceeded to beat his brains out and spill them over the car floor.[52]

"The lights in the car were out, and I went to turn them on. We then got in the far end of the car and waited for the other man to come. Trousdale was armed with the dead man's rifle, and I had my gun, which was in the car. We sat there for more than an hour waiting for the man to come. I was on a pile of boxes higher up than Trousdale, who was near the door in the opposite end of the car from the place where he had brained the first man. Finally, the second robber came nosing through the door to see where his partner had gone. We both blazed away at him but Trousdale got him with the rifle, and he was a dead one."[53]

Both J. K. Regan and David Trousdale believe the third person waiting for the two bandits to return for their rides escaped into the hills after hearing the shots. Some speculated that Laura Bullion was the accomplice holding their horses, but there wasn't any evidence to link her to the crime.[54]

Where Laura Bullion disappeared to between 1912 and 1917 is unknown. She turned up in Memphis, Tennessee, in 1918 claiming to be a widow. She told people her husband, Maurice Lincoln, had been killed fighting overseas in World War I. The quiet woman found employment as a seamstress for various department stores.[55]

Laura Bullion, the last member of the West's most notorious outlaw gang and the last known woman to ever help rob a train, died on December 2, 1961. She was laid to rest in Memphis Memorial Park Cemetery. She was eighty-five years old.[56]

CHAPTER 5

Lillie Langtry:
The Jersey Lily and the LaLee

A HUGE CLOUD OF STEAM BOILED OUT OF THE TREMENDOUS STACK ON the locomotive engine hauling a Union Pacific train up a steep grade outside Colorado Springs, Colorado, in 1888. Among the many cars being pulled along was one belonging to the celebrated actress Lillie Langtry. The seventy-five-foot, blue, private car named the LaLee was the theatrical star's home away from home as she toured the United States performing at various theaters. The LaLee was designed by Colonel William D'Alton Mann, the inventor of the Mann Boudoir Railway Carriage, a rival of the Pullman coach. Mann, who was infatuated with the talented beauty, offered to create a luxurious car for her in the summer of 1887. In early 1888, his plans were submitted to the construction company Harlan and Hollingworth in Wilmington, Delaware, and the building of the LaLee began shortly thereafter.[1]

Born in 1853 on the Isle of Jersey, a few miles off the coast of Saint-Malo, France, Lillie was tall and curvaceous with azure eyes and Titian red hair. She had been the toast of Great Britain, a professional beauty. Eminent portrait painters and photographers asked her to sit for them. Poets recited blank verse about her arresting features.[2] In America, Lillie had captured audiences with both her looks and acting ability. She had been performing at venues in the East just prior to her private car being completed. The moment the vehicle was ready to travel, Lillie and her entourage climbed aboard for a journey west, where she was scheduled to appear at the Louis' Opera House in San Diego.[3]

The famous actress Lillie Langtry traveled across America in her own private railroad car she named the LaLee. LIBRARY OF CONGRESS

The railway car, which Lillie christened LaLee (Winnebago, Native American for Flirt), cost sixty-five thousand dollars and bore a striking resemblance to Cleopatra's barge. "I think the Colonel thoroughly enjoyed planning the car," Lillie wrote later in her life. "Being very hard at work rehearsing a new play, I let him have his lead, and, beyond an occasional letter with reference to color or material, he did not disturb me with details, so that, when the finished car and the bill for it burst on my view almost simultaneously, I am not sure whether joy at possessing such a beautiful perambulating home or honor at my extravagance in ordering it was uppermost in my mind."[4]

The LaLee was an attention getter. The exterior of the car was a cobalt blue, Lillie's favorite color, and on either side were emblazoned wreaths of golden lilies encircling its name. The roof was white, and there was an unusual quantity of decorative brass, wrought into conventional designs of lilies, and the massive platforms were of polished teak from India. Most railroad travelers were awestruck by Lillie Langtry's private car, but not everyone took notice of the LaLee. For some, it was merely a means of getting from one place to another. An example of such an attitude occurred during the first extended trip Lillie took with the car. As the train was leaving Colorado Springs, two men ran down the tracks in hopes of hitching a ride to the next station. The car they hopped aboard was the LaLee. They stood on the back platform of the car watching the scenery, blissfully unaware to whom it belonged.[5]

After traveling a few miles, Lillie's porter, Ben, noticed the men on the platform and invited them to walk through the LaLee to the public coaches. They were about to accept when the porter explained to them to go quickly as the car was a private one and occupied by a lady. At this piece of news, the men stolidly declined to enter the car at all, declaring that they had been living for years in the mountains without seeing a woman and had no desire to renew the acquaintance with the opposite sex.[6]

Lillie overheard the exchange and peaked around the door to get a look at the men. "Ben tried in vain to break their determination," Lillie noted in her memoirs, but the men remained steadfast. "They stood their guns and did not budge until the train drew up at a lonely wayside station," Lillie continued, "when they dropped off and entered the smoker ahead, thus it is to be hoped, securing immunity from what they evidently regarded as the feminine peril."[7]

If the men had ventured through the LaLee, they would have seen the interior of the car was as impressive as the exterior. According to Lillie, "The designer certainly devised a wonderful sleeping room and bath. The sleeping room was upholstered in Nile green silk brocade, was entirely padded, ceiling, walls, dressing table, etc., with the idea of protecting the passengers in case of a collision. The bath and its fittings were of silver, and the curtains of both rooms, of rose-colored silk, were trimmed with profusion of lace. The saloon was large, and upholstered in cream and green brocade," Lillie wrote in her memoirs. "It was made specifically for the LaLee in Lyons, and I was agreeably surprised to find a piano installed therein. There were two guest rooms, a maid's room, complete even with a sewing machine, a pantry, a kitchen, and sleeping quarters for the staff.[8]

"Underneath were enormous ice-chests capable of housing a whole stag, as I discovered later. For extra safety, Colonel Mann had furnished the LaLee with thirteen floors and eleven ceilings, which comforting precautions, together with the huge refrigerators, made the car so heavy that I was more than once officially warned to avoid semi-tottering bridges."[9]

The scene at the train depots was always the same when Lillie and the LaLee arrived. Fans eager for her arrival in San Diego, where she was to perform at the Louis' Opera House on May 4, 1888, congregated at the city's depot to greet her. Newspaper reporters were on hand to witness the scene. From the moment the train stopped, "the crowd strained for a glimpse of the actress alighting from her car," an article in the May 6, 1888, edition of the *Los Angeles Herald* read. "Her appearance will mark a new era in the amusement record of San Diego." The crowd pushed forward to admire the LaLee and to stare at the teakwood doors in antici-pation of their opening. Hours passed, and the rose-colored curtains that covered the stained-glass windows of Lillie's portable palace remained drawn. The intrepid thespian would not leave the car until it was time to relocate to the dressing area at the theater. Until Lillie's followers had the

A look at the restroom on the LaLee. LIBRARY OF CONGRESS

pleasure of seeing her on stage, they had to be content with the fact that they did have a chance to see the LaLee.[10]

From the time the LaLee began the journey west with the actress nicknamed "the Jersey Lily," people clamored for information about the stylish car. In late February 1888, the train pulling the private car stopped in Chicago, where Lillie was to be performing in the play *The Lady of Lyons*. A story in the February 21, 1888, edition of the *Chicago Tribune* covered Lantry's arrival and made mention of the opulent vehicle in which she lived. The headline read, "Mrs. Langtry Suddenly Taken Ill and Is Confined to Her Car." The article that followed explained the situation. "There was a forlorn air about the parlor-car LaLee as it lay huddled up last night in the yard of the Union Depot. It seemed it was all on one side, all disheveled, all disordered. On the rear platform there was a dreary litter of empty champagne cases; and on the front platform there hung before the door a red plush sign, 'Not at Home.'[11]

"LaLee [believed by some reporters that the LaLee and Lillie were one and the same] was not at home. And in fact, at the present time she was in no mood either to flirt or to occupy herself with any diversion at all. She was ill with neuralgia of the heart, complicated with rheumatism, and she lay in her little sleeping room, which looks like a ship's cabin, tossing restlessly under the coverlet of violet silk.[12]

" 'Yes,' she said wearily. 'I am really ill. I was ill all last week and found it difficult to act. But I thought it would pass. I sent a telegraph to Dr. Irwin. I wanted to be ready in case of need. I was fairly well yesterday. Charles Coghlan and some friends came to supper. They will tell you I was in good spirits all the time and had no thought of this collapse. The Dr. arrived this morning. He said at once that I was overworked. 'Very much run down', were his words. He also said there were symptoms of neuralgia of the heart. These developed about 6:30 this evening. I was dressing for the theatre over there by the looking-glass, when I suddenly felt giddy, staggered back, and said: 'Send for Dr. Irwin, I am very ill.' Then I lay on the bed until the doctor came. He at once wrote the following certificate. 'This is to certify that Mrs. Langtry is so ill that it is impossible for her to appear at the theatre this evening. She has just attempted to

Lillie Langtree's LaLee was elegantly furnished. In addition to the custom-made chairs, the car carried a piano for the actress to practice playing. AUTHOR'S COLLECTION

dress, contrary to my services, and fainted. I now consider it my duty to insist on absolute quiet for the present. J. A. Irwin, M.D.'"[13]

On April 12, 1888, Lillie's car was the subject of an article in the *St. Joseph Gazette-Herald*. Mrs. Langtry's health had long since been restored by the time the article was published. "Lillie Langtry's special car LaLee built for her by the Mann Boudoir Car company, at the cost of $25,000,* will be an object of interest in the vicinity of the depot on Monday next. The walls and ceiling of Mrs. Langtry's boudoir are upholstered in olive green satin, the elaborate frieze being relieved by a round border of satin. The bed, which occupies the entire width of the room, is screened by curtains of pink satin, and covered by a counterpane of the same material, embroidered in the center with the initial L. Between the windows is a dressing-case with mirror, supplied with silver and ivory toilet parapher-nalia. The car is finished in the most elaborate and luxurious manner, and in excellent taste."[14]

Lillie relished traveling in her own car. According to her memoirs, she enjoyed the "American method of travel" and marveled at the beauty

---

* The cost of the car's construction listed here is inaccurate.

of the country. "The glory of the autumn coloring in America is indescribable," Lillie wrote in her memoirs. "The apple orchards of New York State, through which we passed, are especially graven on my memory. Mounds of fresh-gathered fruit, some golden, some crimson, lay about the trees, many of which still carried their colorful burden. Certain marvels, such as Niagara, were too awesome to be appreciated at once, but perhaps the first glimpse of the Yosemite Valley, from the top of the hill was the most soul-stirring of all of them. The Mariposa Grove of big trees filled me with an almost childish astonishment."[15]

During the time Lillie toured the country in the LaLee, the train and subsequent car were not involved in a single accident. The actress noted that the LaLee did, however, experience one or two narrow escapes. "While going south, the couplings gave way unperceived," she shared in her memoirs, "and the LaLee was left standing for two hours on a single line in a magnolia forest, but, until an engine returned in burning haste to fetch us, the occupants of the car had been sleeping in blissful ignorance of its jeopardy.[16]

"On one or two occasions we jolted off the line, one of these mishaps occurring near a small Texas town. There was necessarily a considerable delay, and the cowboys lounging around the station improvised a rodeo or exhibition of prowess for my entertainment.[17]

"There were times the heavy LaLee could not make it up the steep inclines in the Sierras without the aid of an additional engine. While waiting for officials at a nearby station in Truckee, California, to send a second engine, some of the railroad employees were summoned to help push the ponderous LaLee up the grade out of harm's way."[18]

In addition to the mechanical issues and challenges the LaLee faced in certain terrain, the car was at the center of a police investigation at one time. In June 1888, Lillie's car was parked at a rail yard in Houston, Texas. After a few days' stay at the location, the train was to press on toward California. An hour or so before daylight, a horse-drawn carriage approached the vehicle. One of the guardsmen aboard the LaLee attempted to stop the driver of the carriage from getting close to the famous actress's sleeping quarters. It was the guardsman's job to protect Lillie and her property. The guardsman leapt off the LaLee and stood in front of the carriage until it came to a stop. The driver was outraged by the behavior, jumped out the vehicle, and began exchanging blows with the guardsman. The guardsman yelled for another security guard to help him, and the man raced to the fight. The driver of the carriage managed to get away from the pair and took his complaint about his treatment to the authorities.[19]

Early the following morning, the police visited the LaLee with a warrant to arrest Lillie's guards. "Mrs. Langtry in her night robes was the first person to open the door when the law came calling," a report in the June 12, 1888, edition of the *Utah Daily Union* read. She had no idea who the men were at first and mistook them as outlaws. " 'O! I have nothing, Mr. Train Robber,' Lillie called out. 'Please don't shoot, I have no money.' This caused a loud laugh, and when informed that they were policemen she seemed much relieved."[20]

The police searched the LaLee for the guardsmen in question, and when they were found, they were arrested. Lillie's truculent champions were brought before the judge and subsequently fined twenty-five dollars for their overly aggressive behavior.[21]

Lillie Langtry had a huge fan base across the United States. Some of her most devoted admirers were politicians, artists, and inventors. Among those who idolized the Jersey Lily was Judge Roy Bean, Texas's justice of the peace and the "Law West of the Pecos." The eccentric judge was so enamored with Lillie, he renamed the town where he lived and held court Langtry. The saloon where he distributed law and order was called the Jersey Lilly. At one time he wrote Lillie to let her know about the section of Texas dedicated to her beauty and talent. The judge invited Lillie to visit Langtry, meet the townspeople, and have a drink at his bar. The celebrated actress was flattered by the gesture.[22]

"The greatest surprise of all was to have a town named in my honor," Lillie recalled in her memoirs. "It was impossible for me to get to Texas at that time, and on writing him my regrets, I offered a present, an ornamental drinking fountain, but Roy Bean's quick reply was that it would be quite useless, as the only thing the citizens of Langtry didn't drink was water.[23]

"Time passed and I came and went and toured, and forgot the circumstances. Then, on a later trip to California [in mid-1903] by the

Southern route, the invitation was repeated by the 'bigwigs' of the township who besought me to take advantage of passing through Langtry to bestow half an hour on a reception. The Southern Pacific was willing, and my company and I awaited the new experience with great excitement, working ourselves up to a high point of interest and anticipation as the train having crossed the Pecos River, sped nearer and nearer to my train.[24]

"The afternoon sun was blazing down on the parched sandy plain with its monotonous clothing of sagebrush and low growing cactus, when the Sunset Express came to a sudden stop. A casual glance from the window of the LaLee revealed no reason why we should pause there rather than at any other point of the continuous grey desert, but the three wooly heads of my devoted staff made a simultaneous appearance in the doorway of the salon, announcing in an excited chorus, the fact that we were actually at Langtry, but, on account of my car being, as usual, placed at the tail end of the long train, we could see no sign of habitation.[25]

"I hurriedly alighted just as a cloud of sand heralded the approach of a numerous throng of citizens ploughing their way the entire length of the train to give me the glad hand."[26]

The residents of Langtry happily welcomed Lillie to the town. Cowboys were dressed in their finest leathers and flamboyant shirts, and the women were adorned in their best blouses, skirts, and bonnets. After the postmaster shared a quick history of the quaint burg, Lillie was escorted to the Jersey Lilly Saloon. "Trudging through several stands of sagebrush and prickly cactus, we arrived at our destination," Lillie later recalled.[27]

"It was a roughly built wooden two-story house, its entire front being shaded by a piazza, on which a chained monkey gamboled, the latter (installed when the saloon was built) bearing the name of 'The Lilly' in my honor. The interior of the 'Ritz' of Langtry consisted of a long narrow room which comprised the entire ground floor, from whence a ladder staircase led to a sleeping loft. One side of the room was given up to a bar, naturally the most important feature of the place—while stoutly made tables and a few benches occupied the vacant space. The tables showed plainly that they had been severely used, for they were slashed as if with Bowie knives, and on each was a well-thumbed deck of playing cards. It was here that Roy Bean, justice of the peace, and self-styled 'law west of the Pecos River,' used to hold his court and administer justice, which, incidentally, sometimes brought 'grist to the mill.' The stories I was told of his ready wit and audacity made me indeed sorry that he had not lived over my visit."[28]

Lillie left the saloon and followed the townspeople to the schoolhouse. The schoolmistress presented her with drawings the children had made, and Lillie graciously accepted them. Before being whisked off toward the cemetery, she promised to send a supply of suitable books for the students. Once the brief tour of Langtry ended, Lillie made her way back to the LaLee. "On nearing the train," Lillie remembered in her memoir, "which was becoming rather impatient, I saw the strange sight of a huge cinnamon bear careening across the line, dragging a cowboy at the end of a long chain. The LaLee was decorated with a good many cages for my journey through the South. I had acquired a jumping frog at Charleston, an alligator in Florida, a number of horned toads, and a delightfully trained prairie dog called Bob. Hence, I suppose, the correct inference was drawn that I was fond of animals, and the boys resolved to add the late Roy Bean's pet to my collection. They hoisted the unwilling animal onto the platform, and tethered him to the rail, but happily, before I had time to rid myself of the unwelcomed addition without seeming discourteous, he broke away, scattered the crowd and caused some of the vaqueros to start shooting wildly at the bear."[29]

"It was a short-lived visit, but an unforgettable one. As a substitute for the run-away bear, I was presented later with Roy Bean's revolver, which hangs in a place of honor in my English home and bears the following inscription: 'Presented by W. H. Dodd of Langtry, Texas, to Miss Lillie Langtry in honor of her visit to our town. The pistol was formerly the property of Judge Roy Bean. It aided him in finding some of his famous decisions and keeping order west of the Pecos River. It also kept order in the Jersey Lilly Saloon. Kindly accept this as a small token of our regards.'"[30]

After her visit in Langtry, Lillie and the LaLee pressed on toward California. She so loved the state that she purchased a four-thousand-acre ranch in Lake County. Lillie and the friends traveling with her to the West Coast accompanied her to San Francisco to purchase furniture for her new home. She recalled the "exhilarating" adventure in her memoirs. "The tour finished and, with the company disbanded, I felt I had earned my holiday, and set off with a party of friends in my private railway car, LaLee, to follow the stacks of furniture which had already preceded me in charge of my English butler, Beverly.[31]

"We started at day-break [to travel to Lake County from San Francisco] and after several hours rail, arrived at the border of a stupendous lake, with ferry boats crossing and recrossing it in every direction. Our whole train, with the exception of the engine, was run on board one of the above and we were ferried across, a proceeding which occupied about an hour. On the other side a little more travel brought us to the railway's end as far as we were concerned. My nearest station, called St. Helena, was a mere village, and my country town was Sacramento, which lay in a beautiful valley about four hundred miles to the southeast.[32]

"The depot was crowded inside and out, the whole countryside being massed to receive me, armed with ubiquitous autograph books and presents of flowers, fruit, and candy and offers of hospitality! There, also, among the quantity of queer-looking wagon and buggies used in those outlandish parts were two private Wild-West coaches commandeered from my ranch, each with six more or less reliable horses attached, and determined-looking drivers in waiting.[33]

"After signing autographs and entertaining many relays of Californians to an informal reception and tea on my car, we clambered on to the antediluvian stage-coaches which were to convey myself and party, bar accidents, to the promised land. The seventeen miles we had to drive led us, by a corkscrew road, up and over one of the highest summits of the group. The way was rough and narrow and, as the only springs of the two coaches were leather thongs, we felt every stone, but the beauty of the well-wooded gorges, green and cool, with rapid rivers hurrying through them, well repaid us for our thumps and bumps. Then, as we descended the mountain on the farther side, the panorama opened out and, for the first time, I caught a bird's eye view of my property.[34]

"The huge plateau appeared a dream of loveliness. Being early July, vast masses of ripe corn waved golden in the light summer breeze, dotted here and there with enormous evergreen oaks. It was, without exaggeration, entrancing. In the distance were the boundary hills of the far side of my land, hazy and blue as the Alps sometimes are. On the down we drove, each turn of the road making us gasp with the new picture disclosed until, threading our way through my vineyards and peach orchards laden with fruit, which covered a great part of the near hills, we reached home."[35]

After five theatrical seasons spent in America, Lillie returned to England to continue her profession. She returned to the States occasionally between 1909 and 1916. The LaLee was housed somewhere near Lillie's ranch. She was able to use the private car in 1909, but, sadly, the LaLee was destroyed by a fire during Lillie's temporary absence. According to her biography, the actress was heartbroken. "After having been a bliss to me through numerous tours, the LaLee was doomed to a sudden and tragic end," Lillie later wrote about the loss.[36]

The LaLee proved to be an effective publicity device for Lillie Langtry. Tens of thousands of words were written about it. It attracted attention everywhere, proudly advertising the presence of its famous owner.

CHAPTER 6

Mary Pennington: The Creator of the Modern Refrigerator Boxcar

"UNDERFEEDING WILL MAKE A COWARD OF A NATION," DR. MARY PENnington announced at the National Poultry, Butter and Egg Association conference in Chicago in October 1917. "A hungry man may rise to a moment of valor, but when a whole people are hungry, they become moral and physical weaklings."

At the time Dr. Pennington made this statement, she was serving as chief of the food research laboratory of the United States Department of Agriculture. America had entered World War I six months prior to the conference in Illinois, and Mary was on a mission to encourage the country's farmers to increase shipments of poultry, eggs, and fish. "The supply of beef is not enough to go around and the deficit must be made up with other food," the October 19, 1917, edition of the *Leavenworth Times* reported the doctor as saying. "We must feed our men in the trenches and the men of our allies. We must also feed the civilians of our own country and those of our allies."[1]

Mary's goal was sound, but the method for transporting meat and produce from one part of the United States to the other without those goods going bad had not yet been perfected. She would spend the next six years working with railroad companies developing the modern refrigerator boxcar.

Mary Engle Pennington was born in 1872 in Nashville, Tennessee. Her parents were Quakers who showered their children with attention and nurtured their academic talents. Mary's interest in chemistry

Dr. Mary Engle Pennington

came about after reading one of her father's books. She knew early in her life she would pursue a career in the field. She entered the University of Pennsylvania in Philadelphia in 1890 with the idea of acquiring a degree in science. Women pursuing a higher education was a relatively new notion. Despite the fact that the university did not grant degrees to women, Mary completed her coursework, receiving high marks in every subject. Officials at the school awarded her a proficiency certificate in chemistry, zoology, and botany. Mary continued with her studies, earning the respect of the board of trustees, who decided to bestow her with an advance PhD in 1895.[2]

From 1897 to 1899, she researched physiological chemistry at Yale. Before she ended her time at the Ivy League institution, she accepted a position as the director of the clinical laboratory with the Women's Medical College of Pennsylvania. During that same period, Mary also served as bacteriologist with the Philadelphia Bureau of Health and worked for the Pennsylvania Department of Hygiene. While with the government agencies, she successfully raised sanitation standards for the handling of milk and milk products.[3]

The research and published findings that came about as a result of Mary's work on bacteria toxicity levels in dairy products caught the attention of Harvey Wiley. Wiley was a chemist and head of the US Department of Agriculture who believed strongly that the country needed to have food safety standards. He had dedicated his efforts to determining what, if any, hazardous effects resulted in adding coloring matter and preservatives to foods and canned goods specifically. Dr. Wiley's work created problems for canning factories where vegetables, fruits, and meats were put up for table use and formed the chief winter diet for a large part of the people of the United States in the early 1900s.[4]

In 1905, Dr. Wiley offered Mary a job on his "poison squad." The squad was made up of like-minded chemists and botanists interested in the idea that consumers should expect the food they purchased to be pure and not filled with chemicals. Wiley believed Mary's vast knowledge about agricultural products in cold storage would greatly benefit the department. Mary joined the team, and their combined discoveries prompted political leaders to approve the Pure Food and Drug Act of

1906. The act forced food manufacturers to list all the ingredients of the product on the package and prohibited the use of ingredients known to be deleterious to human health.[5]

Not long after the passage of the act, Dr. Wiley asked Mary to head the Bureau of Chemistry's Food Research Lab. In anticipation that the hiring of a woman to such a lofty title might not be well received, Dr. Wiley presented Mary's résumé, under the name of M. E. Pennington, and credentials to the executive who reviewed potential civil service employees. Mary was hired. Her job was to help implement the Pure Food and Drug Act. Under her leadership, the laboratory conducted pioneering research leading to the recognition that fresh foods could keep much longer without spoiling when they were kept at low temperatures.[6]

In a presentation given to the Warehousemen's Association in Washington, DC, on October 3, 1908, Mary explained the importance of cooling fruits immediately upon their being picked and warned the association that all food products should be merely cooled and kept cool and not frozen. She demonstrated that freezing food products caused chemical changes that materially altered the nature of the product. She also discussed the cooling of milk and butter and showed that the careful manufacture in the latter was of equal importance to care in transportation.[7]

A cold-storage boxcar, built under the direction of the Agricultural Department, was exhibited at the conference, and Mary gave a detailed explanation of the capabilities of the car. "This unit can create a temperature of fifteen degrees below zero and is intended to be used at fruit groves in cooling off the fruits as they are picked in order that they may get to market in perfect condition," the December 4, 1908, edition of the *Washington Post* quoted her at the Warehousemen's Association. The car was scheduled to be sent to California to be tested by actual use in the orange and lemon groves during the harvest season and then taken to Florida. Mary would travel with the car and carry out experiments along the way.[8]

The first refrigerated boxcars, or "reefers" as they were called, became part of the railroad's rolling stock in the late 1860s. Early designs featured metal racks that extended across the width of the car in which beef and pork were hung above a frozen mixture of ice and salt. The design was

Dr. Pennington conducting experiments on refrigeration railway boxcars
UNIVERSITY ARCHIVES AND RECORDS CENTER, UNIVERSITY OF PENNSYLVANIA

improved upon in 1875. Huge blocks of ice were packed into cars, and additional ice was added along the route via hatches in the roof. Hay and sawdust were packed around the ice to give it added insulation. Screen slats on opposite sides of the hatches on the roof provided the necessary ventilation. The train's motion circulated the cool air throughout the cargo space. Meat and produce shipped cross-country risked contamination and mold using those inefficient, rudimentary refrigerator cars. Mary was convinced that improvements made to the refrigerator boxcar would keep perishable food making its way from one coast to the other from rotting. Inventing such a mechanism would help farmers and livestock growers increase their business, enable railroad companies to expand their lines, and keep consumers of these goods and services healthy.[9]

In addition to working on designing a refrigerator boxcar, Mary was tasked with educating the public about the benefits of cold storage. Housewives across the country in 1910 were opposed to buying frozen foods, particularly poultry. The prevailing thought was that the product wasn't fresh. Whenever they did purchase a frozen chicken, most women were placing it in water or leaving it outside in a pan to thaw. That action contaminated the food and made people who ate the chicken sick. The recommended thawing process was to take place in a home refrigerator over a period of time.[10]

"No housewife can afford nowadays to remain in ignorance of what has happened to her chicken before she buys it," Dr. Pennington explained in an article titled "A Woman's Work for Pure Storage Food," in the March 20, 1910, edition of the *Oregon Daily Journal*. "What will happen afterwards is too direct a consequence of what has happened previously. The investigation which began with the study of poultry in cold storage, developed the impressive, guiding fact about four years ago that the condition of poultry when it came out depended largely on its condition when it went in.[11]

"Every detail in the handling of perishable food products is important, and the underlying principle is the same whether storage is dealing with an apple or a carload of chicken. The chicken that is exhibited to the marketing housewife on the butcher's stall is a chicken, it is true, but it is most likely not to be the particular era of chicken that it seems. And between the period when it was a live chicken and the period when it makes its public debut as dead, one of the fates of many elements have worked their will upon it.[12]

"For some of its mischances, the housewife herself is responsible. It is therefore fitting that, as women have done so much to afflict the modern supply of poultry, a woman should be the one to study out the remedies," Dr. Pennington concluded.[13]

"Perhaps a mere man, not endowed with woman's native affinity for chickens, might have been able to conduce the cold-storage investigations successfully, in spite of the handicap of his sex," the *Oregon Daily Journal* article continued. "But the fact is simply that mere man didn't and that Dr. Pennington's previous record marked her for the expert whom Secretary Wilson and Dr. Wiley wanted on the job.[14]

"She took her degree as doctor of philosophy at the University of Pennsylvania, and has since carried on investigations in chemistry and bacteriology in connection with both public and private laboratories. The importance and the urgent public need of the government inquiry into the food supply of the people at large became so considerable that she relinquished all her other work to act as the food research expert under Dr. Wiley in the Department of Agriculture.[15]

"The purpose of Dr. Pennington's work was fundamentally, of course, about insuring the perfect food supply to the people at large. But the entire trade and all its allies realized the commercial advantages of the improved methods the government is seeking to discover and establish. Packers, cold-storage warehousemen, merchants, retailers, and far from least on the list, railroad companies—all have cooperated as heartily and helpfully as the most enthusiastic could desire."[16]

Mary conducted her experiments and testing of refrigerator boxcars from a special railcar connected behind the refrigerator boxcar. From her rolling laboratory, she tested food being transported under typical railroad conditions as well as monitored the car's temperature and humidity. Her research revealed that the refrigerator boxcar's insulation was too thin and that the method of construction allowed cracks to form in the exterior shell, leaving what little insulation there was exposed to the outside elements.[17]

After weeks of analyses, Mary determined that the keys to superior refrigerator boxcars were insulation and the need for a forced-air system to maximize air circulation in the car. "Correct insulation," Dr. Pennington noted in an article from the August 17, 1930, edition of the *Atlanta Constitution*, "means walls made with several thicknesses of material between which is packed an insulator of recognized efficiency. This insulating material should completely surround the box, especially protecting joints, seams and corners. The outside of the box may be made of wood or metal, either of which should be both attractive and easily cleaned. The inside of the refrigerator requires a material which is impervious to the moisture and action of constant cleaning methods. A finish on the inside to absorb odors or hold moisture would develop improper sanitation and become a health menace. The hard, enameled, metal linings have proven extremely satisfactory. These should be made with as few seams as possible, so food cannot lodge in cracks and crevices. The necessary seams should be well protected."[18]

Using Mary's research, railroad construction companies implemented the recommended changes. The creation of the modern refrigerator boxcar had a significant impact on the American economy. This technology eliminated the need to transport livestock, which required feed and hands

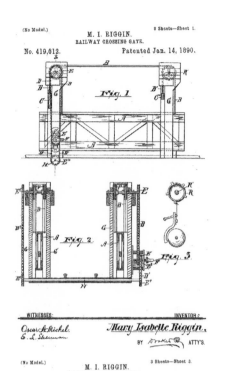

M. I. RIGGIN.
RAILWAY CROSSING GATE.

No. 419,612.   Patented Jan. 14, 1890.

Fig. 1

Fig. 2

Fig. 3

WITNESSES: INVENTOR:

Oscar A. Michel.   *Mary Isabelle Riggin.*
E. L. Sherman.   BY   ATTY'S.

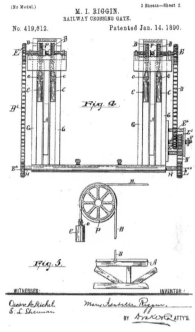

M. I. RIGGIN.
RAILWAY CROSSING GATE.

No. 419,612.   Patented Jan. 14, 1890.

Fig. 4

Fig. 5

WITNESSES: INVENTOR:

Oscar A. Michel.   *Mary Isabelle Riggin.*
E. L. Sherman.   BY   ATTY'S.

M. I. RIGGIN.
RAILWAY CROSSING GATE.

No. 419,612.   Patented Jan. 14, 1890.

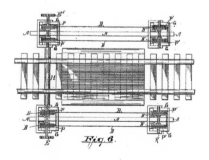

Fig. 6.

Like Dr. Pennington, Mary Isabella Riggins worked on inventions for the betterment of the railroad industry. On this page are the patent drawings for Riggins's Railway Crossing Gate. She was awarded her patent on January 14, 1890. AUTHOR'S COLLECTION

WITNESSES: INVENTOR:

Oscar A. Michel.   *Mary Isabelle Riggin.*
E. L. Sherman.   BY   ATTY'S.

to man the herd. With refrigerator cars, only the parts of the animal in demand needed to be shipped. Meat packing plants that could afford to build their own refrigerator cars to ship their product everywhere and icing services that provided the ice needed for the cars profited substantially. Consumers, too, reaped the reward from the reefers. More foods were made available and affordable to them.[19]

Railroad lines anticipating the additional business ordered a fleet of refrigerator boxcars. According to the January 19, 1922, edition of the *Salina Daily Union*, the Union Pacific Railroad requested bids for thirty-three thousand refrigerator boxcars.[20]

Mary resigned her position at the Bureau of Chemistry's Food Research Lab in 1922 and went to work for the American Balsa Company. While with the bureau, she had discovered that balsa wood was the perfect insulation to be used in refrigerator boxcars and wanted to explore other like areas where balsa could be of service. Mary explained to fellow chemists at a meeting in Scranton, Pennsylvania, in June 1921, that balsa was a tropical tree that weighed a little more than seven pounds per cubic foot as compared with the twenty-five-pound weight of a block of spruce of equal size. "It possesses wonderful heat resisting qualities and is extremely valuable in the construction of refrigerators of all types," she told her peers.[21]

Dr. Mary Pennington's career in cold storage spanned more than thirty years and earned her the nickname "Ice Woman." In addition to designing the modern refrigerator boxcar, she invented a process for scaling, skinning, quick-freezing, and dry-packing fish.[22]

Dr. Pennington died on December 27, 1952, at the age of eighty.[23]

CHAPTER 7

Miriam Leslie: The Journalist Riding the Rails

IT WAS A GLOOMY, CHILLY EVENING IN MID-APRIL 1877 WHEN MIRIAM Leslie; her husband, Frank; a Skye terrier named Follette; and ten of the Leslies' friends and their families gathered at the New York Central Railroad depot in New York City. Porters carefully serpentined around crates of fruits, vegetables, spices, and vintage red wine until they reached the area of the loading dock where the travelers' expensive trunks, leather hat boxes, and gold-embossed luggage were waiting. The parade of baggage handlers scooped up the cargo and carried it aboard.[1]

Stylishly dressed men and women congregated around the platform leading to the passenger car like moths circling a bright light. They conversed excitedly with one another about the impending trip as the train belched a steady stream of steam into the air. They pretended not to notice the activity about them and blithely sipped champagne served to them by valets wearing white gloves and adorned in waistcoats.[2]

At twenty minutes past eight, Miriam Leslie climbed the steps of a magnificent coach, turned to the crowd, and raised her glass in a toast to all assembled. She called their attention to the name scrolled across the side of the coach, which read Wagner Sleeping Car. The group applauded approvingly, and then Miriam announced, "Ladies and gentlemen, I give you the inventor of this extraordinary coach, Senator Webster Wagner." Another round of applause was offered as the distinguished, gray-haired statesman gave a quick bow and waved at those showing their appreciation for his work.[3]

Mrs. Frank Leslie—Miriam to friends and family ACCESSIBLE ARCHIVES, INC., 5 GREAT VALLEY PARKWAY, MALVERN, PA 19355, 866-296-1488, FRANK LESLIE'S WEEKLY, ACCESSIBLE ARCHIVES MARKETING WEB PAGE, PICTURE WITH CAPTION, MIRIAM FLORENCE LESLIE. HTTP://WWW.ACCESSIBLE-ARCHIVES.COM

The Wagner sleeping and parlor cars were each forty feet long. Thick, olive-colored curtains and silk shades accentuated the rows of windows that lined the coach; chandeliers painted with elaborate designs hung from the ceilings. The walls were covered in a rich, dark walnut, the seating was covered in plush upholstery, and the fixtures were brass. Small washrooms bookended the parlor car. The sleep car was lavish, with plush, comfortable seats that unfolded into sleeping berths and privacy partitions made from mulberry silk.[4]

Miriam and Frank had commissioned Wagner to construct the luxurious cars for the purpose of transporting the magazine publisher, his wife, and several of their friends across the country from New York to San Francisco. When the train whistle blew, the ten members of the Leslies' party said their good-byes to those who had come to see them off on the journey and boarded the passenger car. The vehicle pulled away from the station at approximately eight thirty in the evening. Another blast of the train whistle announced the official departure to points west.[5]

The long-distance excursion was covered in the April 18, 1877, edition of the *San Francisco Examiner*. According to the report, the tour would take six weeks from start to finish. "The party includes one or two artists," the article noted, "and having engaged a palace car with the privilege to 'switch off' when and where they please, they will stop whenever a bit of scenery promises to prove of interest or worth sketching. It is to be hoped, too, that we shall have some pen pictures as a result of this journey. Mrs. Frank Leslie, besides being a brilliant conversationalist, wields a very charming pen, and a look at California through her spectacles would be racy and artistic." Miriam had every intention of recording what she experienced on the trip in her memoir.[6]

Miriam Florence Folline was born in New Orleans on June 5, 1836, to aristocratic parents who appreciated travel. She grew up with an eye toward seeing the world. Miriam's father, Charles, was away from home a great deal when she was growing up, and tales of his business ventures and visits to various parts of the country fueled her desire to embark on as many journeys as possible. Her family moved to New York when Miriam was a young girl. She attended the finest schools and learned to speak several languages, including German and Spanish.[7]

Considered by most to be "attractive in both mind and body," Miriam never lacked for male companionship. Her first romantic encounter ended in scandal when a jeweler's clerk named David Peacock took a fancy to the stunning teenager. Miriam would visit Mr. Peacock at the jewelry store where he worked and persuaded him to let her borrow several pieces of the shop's inventory to wear about town. When her mother, Susan, learned of her behavior, she was furious. She believed Peacock's actions compromised her daughter's virtue and demanded he marry Miriam. Conditions were made by Charles and Susan prior to the union. Miriam would not be allowed to live with Peacock. She would remain at home, and Peacock would financially support her. After a discreet amount of time, the marriage was annulled.[8]

Miriam's older brother, actor Augustus Noel, also known as Frank Folline, was involved in a sordid romance of his own at the time, one that would ultimately benefit his sister. Augustus had traveled west in 1854 with the gold rush and, during a stay in Grass Valley, California, met the notorious entertainer Lola Montez. Lola and Augustus fell in love, and she hired him to be a part of her stage show scheduled to tour Australia. The pair, as well as the rest of the troupe, set sail for the country in early June 1855 from San Francisco. A year later they returned to America via the same route but were caught up in a storm prior to reaching the California coast. Augustus fell overboard and was drowned. Lola was heartbroken and blamed herself for the accident. In a letter to the Folline family, the entertainer expressed her sadness and invited Miriam to consider joining her in her stage show. Lola had seen a picture of Miriam while with Augustus and raved about her beauty. Lola believed Miriam's looks would attract an audience. Miriam happily accepted the offer to tour with the famous woman known as the Countess of Landsfeld. The chance to see the world would finally be realized.[9]

Miriam traveled with Lola Montez's troupe for more than a year. She gained a host of admirers at each venue she appeared. Her followers included wealthy bankers, celebrities, and politicians. She was a much-sought-after guest at many important functions in New York and Washington. In the fall of 1857, Miriam met archaeologist, railroad president, and newspaper editor Ephraim G. Squier. The couple wed in October 1857. Together, the Squiers journeyed from one location to the next, meeting with dignitaries, dining with royalty from foreign countries, and attending political events such as President Abraham Lincoln's inaugural ball. It was at that ball that the twenty-nine-year-old Miriam met Frank

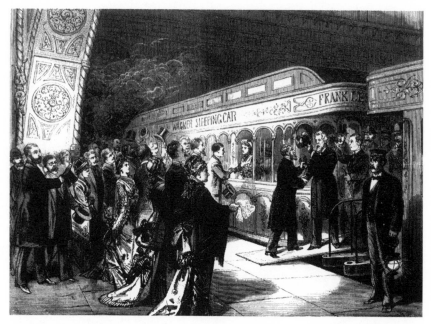

The start of the Frank Leslie transcontinental trip on April 10, 1877 ACCESSIBLE ARCHIVES, INC., 5 GREAT VALLEY PARKWAY, MALVERN, PA 19355, 866-296-1488, FRANK LESLIE'S WEEKLY, ONLINE DATABASE, PICTURE WITH CAPTION, PAGE 140, APRIL 28, 1877 ISSUE. HTTP://WWW.ACCESSIBLE-ARCHIVES.COM/

Leslie, the man who owned the paper where her husband was soon to be employed.[10]

Miriam and Frank were instantly taken with one another, and although both were married to other people, the two began a passionate affair. After Miriam shared with Frank that Ephraim was struggling with his businesses, particularly the railroad, Frank offered Ephraim a job as editor of his illustrated newspaper. Miriam was then named editor of the *Leslie Lady's Magazine*. She excelled at the position, contributing numerous articles about life and travel. In a short time, Miriam was editing several of Frank's many publications.[11]

By mid-1873, after being involved in an affair for more than eight years, both Miriam and Frank divorced their spouses and were free to marry each other. The couple wed on May 31, 1873, and purchased a new home in New York on Fifth Avenue. The new Mrs. Frank Leslie wasted no time establishing herself among the most elite in New York society. She was, however, no more faithful to her third husband than she had been to the second. American poet and frontiersman Joaquin Miller and Miriam began a thirty-year affair shortly after the Leslies' honeymoon ended.[12]

Although Miriam had taken advantage of the many opportunities to visit destinations around the world with her husbands and lovers, travel continued to excite her. Embarking on a cross-country trip in specially designed railroad carriages with good friends and the promise of witnessing some of America's most beautiful locations gave Miriam a thrill. She was eager to report on the excursion in future editions of *Leslie's Illustrated Newspaper*. She hoped those reports would promote train travel and encourage readers to take to the rails.[13]

When the members of the Leslie party first stepped into the Wagner coaches, they were pleasantly surprised by the opulent interior. Once the guests adjusted themselves to the pristine setting, they agreed to refer to the palace car simply as "home." "And very soon after reaching such a decision," Miriam explained in her journal, "the car assumed the pleasant aspect suggested by the word, as the bouquets, shawls, rugs, sofa-cushions, and various personalities of the three ladies of the party were developed and arranged upon or around a table in the central division of the car, which was to represent the general salon, our end being partitioned off by curtains to serve as bowers for such of the party as had given hostages to society in the shape of husband or wife; while the other end, also screened by curtains, became a pleasant Bohemia where the artists, litterateurs and photographers of the party sleep and work."[14]

The Leslie excursion's first significant scenic stop was Niagara Falls. Harry, also known as Henry Ogden, sketched a view of the falls from Prospect Point. His artwork was included with Miriam's description of the sight she wrote in her book about the trip west.[15]

"The first impressions of Niagara depended much upon the approach, crossing the high suspension bridge of the railroad, a few miles below, the traveler experiences a feeling of disappointment; the height of the fall is diminished by the perspective. But when he comes to view it from a lower level, this disappointment is overcome by surprise at the sudden growth of the gigantic torrent.[16]

"As we came toward it, we first saw a narrow strip of lazy, smooth, slow water of the deepest blue, just flecked here and there with streaks of foam, slipping away between steep gray walls of rock, not unlike the palisades of the Hudson; a light bridge is then seen spanning the straight, clean-cut groove; now we catch the first sight of white pouring water, solid and immense, and a cloud of dense white steam hanging over the narrow blue river at what seems to be its source.[17]

"We are here between seasons. Winter is the season for Niagara—summer for visitors. But Niagara at all seasons is indescribably magnificent."[18]

Miriam's pleasure trip from Gotham to the Golden Gate was covered by newspapers across the country. At every important point along the route, stops were made and photographs were taken of the Leslies and their traveling companions.[19] Articles about their visits to Toledo, Ohio; Elkhart, Indiana; and Chicago, Illinois, were well publicized. According to the April 13, 1877, edition of the *Chicago Tribune*, the Leslies and party "arrived via a special car over the Michigan Southern Railway from New York. The party will remain until Sunday morning when they take their departure for Omaha in a special car over the Northwestern Road."[20]

Miriam offered her own report about their arrival in the Windy City and what was to come. She was particularly taken with Chicago. After dining at the Grand Pacific Hotel, Miriam and her entourage toured the town. "We found the fashionable avenues, Wabash, Calmut, Prairie and Michigan, wide, straight, and interesting as drives, from the number and diversity of handsome private dwellings, generally detached, and built in all varieties of styles and ornamentation; even the frame buildings are costly and ornate, and the brick richly decorated with brown-stone copings and carvings. A favorite material, also, is a soft, creamy, yellow stone, similar to that so popular in Paris, and, possibly, the association, recalling the good-natured satire that good Chicagoeans, when they die, go to Paris, may have added to the pleasing effect."[21]

When Miriam and company departed the Windy City on April 16, 1877, they abandoned their Wagner coaches for the stylish Pullman hotel cars. The plush car named the "President" was designed for extended trips over steel rails. The extravagant conveyance was previously used by the emperor of Brazil, Dom Pedro II, in the spring of 1876 to travel across the country and then was placed on exhibit at the Philadelphia Centennial in 1876. Frank Leslie arranged to have the car waiting for Miriam and their companions at the depot of the Chicago and North Western Railway.[22]

"While our party was viewing the exterior of the vehicle," Miriam later wrote, "Mr. George Pullman himself strolled up. Pointing to his wheels, he made the somewhat alarming announcement that they were made of paper! In proportion to its weight, he said, good paper, properly prepared, is one of the strongest substances in the world. It offers equal resistance to fracture in all directions. While the toughest woods are sometimes liable to crack and split under severe trial, and ordinary iron becomes brittle from the constant jarring on the smoothest of steel rails, paper possesses a certain amount of elasticity very desirable in a car wheel. Paper wheels, he said, were subjected to an enormous hydraulic pressure and, when surrounded with a flange of steel, were the most perfect wheels yet invented.[23]

"The excursionists were ushered into the interior of the 'President,' where every comfort is provided. A spacious salon, through the magic of a drop curtain, can be made sitting room, smoking room, drawing room, and retiring room at pleasure. Whatever one longs for in his own house is procurable. The kitchen is a gem of its kind, with every convenience from a mammoth roaster to a charcoal broiler. Pots, kettles, pans, and knives are ranged around the apartment in perfect order. It is located in the rear of the car, and two large tanks suspended from the roof are supplied with water from the outside by means of a hose. Our cook was an artist in his line, and dyspepsia and indigestion were obsolete terms on board the 'President.'"[24]

Between April 16 and April 21, 1877, the Leslies and their associates had traveled over the rolling hills and vast prairies of Iowa and Nebraska and through the Black Hills of South Dakota. While en route to Wyoming, the sojourners came upon the aftermath of a blizzard that had overtaken the area. "We passed through our first snowshed," Miriam recorded in her journal. "[It was] very like a covered bridge or wooden tunnel in effect, and were informed that the Union Pacific Railroad had been obliged to construct hundreds of miles of these, and stone fences at different points of the road, to obviate the drifting snow banks, capable of not only detaining, but of burying, a train."[25]

The party reached Cheyenne, Wyoming, on April 21, 1877. Miriam and her friends had been told that the town was filled with men and women of dubious reputation with a pension for stealing. The group was hesitant at first about leaving the safety of the car. They decided to venture out only if an armed guard accompanied them.[26]

"With a dash of grim, suggestive humor, purely Western, Cheyenne was dubbed in its infancy 'Hell on Wheels'," Miriam recalled in her memoir. "Probably it no longer deserves this title; but in spite of its fine churches and its peaceful and law-abiding populace, one cannot but suspect that the devil has still a lien on the town. Our first study of its distinctive features is by moonlight and lamplight that creates giant shadows and throws only feeble glimmers by way of illumination; a Dore-ish sort of effect, wherein every careless street lounger takes on the aspect of a prowling assassin and the very dogs are clothed in mystery. The street lamps are infinitesimally few and far between, and the lights hung out from shops and saloons are chiefly in the way of lurid red and blue transparencies. Every ten paces one is confronted by a luminous sign with the legend 'Faro' or 'Keno' in great white letters; or that this is the 'Monte Saloon' and that is the 'Arcade' or the 'Montana.' Plenty of loungers around these doorways watch us as we pass: savage-looking miners, high-booted and shaggy-haired; typical 'roughs,' with big dogs lurking at their heels; scouts in buckskin; and here and there a boy in blue from Fort Carlin or Russell, three miles north of the town. The sidewalks are crowded with such vagabond strollers; but it is an orderly crowd, and there is little noise and no visible drunkenness, although it seems to the casual observer that every second house hangs out the sign of a barroom."[27]

From Cheyenne, Miriam and company pressed on toward Colorado. The group stopped in Denver and boarded horse-drawn carriages in order to see the downtown area of the city. The women in the party visited the spacious stores and purchased fineries from the sophisticated array of dresses and hats available. In the evening, Miriam and friends dined with members of the Colorado legislature. "These gentlemen, almost without exception, impressed us not only as men of strength, purpose, and ability, but conspicuous for that genial heartiness of manner, and the gentle kindness of feeling which make the Western gentleman a new and charming type," Miriam noted in her daily journal. "Without trenching too far on private grounds, one may venture, perhaps, to say, that never was this genial manner and fine feeling better exemplified than in the Governor of the Centennial State."[28]

The Leslie party's congenial hosts were equally taken with the visitors from the East and were anxious to show them more of the state in which they were so proud. The morning after the meal with the politicians, the entourage was escorted on a jaunt to Colorado Springs.[29]

"We took passage upon the narrow-gauge railway called the Denver and Rio Grande, running south from that city, and immediately began the steady upward grade by which it climbs the 'divide' between the South Platte and Arkansas Rivers," Miriam explained in her memoir. "At the highest point lies Summit Lake, in the shadow of a great Sugarloaf Mountain, with a background of purple foothills and the snows of Pike's Peak. The waters of this little lake run impartially north and south, and in descending we soon bade goodbye to the snow, and welcomed the buffalo grass and cactus plants telling of a higher temperature. We saw ourselves surrounded on every side by their weird, fantastic forms—turrets, winged castles, needle-like shafts, heaped piles that might have been the home of ghoul or sprite of the desert, and detached columns of red sandstone of every height and proportion, from a toadstool to a Corinthian pillar.[30]

"Colorado Springs, presumably so called because the Springs are five miles away, is not without attractions. There are five roads leading away from it; Pike's Peak looks condescendingly down on it. The air is said to be excellent for asthmatics, who therefore abound here; and its morals are guarded by the sternest of liquor laws."[31]

The experience the party had in Utah was as exhilarating as the scenic encounter they'd had in Colorado. "Round cape like projections and through steep walls of red sandstone, our train goes winding, swinging from side to side like a ship among the waves," Miriam shared in her memoir. "At the very gateway of Echo Canyon, on the crest of a great hill north of the track, is a weatherworn ruin all built in crumbling red stone. They call it 'Castle Rock.' Its doorway is the mouth of a cave one hundred fifty feet deep, and its columns are the work of no meaner architects than Nature and Time themselves. But nothing we have seen along the way is more suggestive of man's planning and execution than this 'Castle Rock,' crowning the summit of a steep divide, overlooking the long descent of the canyon and the winding road crawling through it.[32]

"And then follow wonders as fast as the minutes chase each other. No one can see them all, far less describe them; there is left on the mind a confusion of huge outlines, colossal bulk, glowing color, and unimaginable shapes. There are needle-like spires, red and gray, carved and fretted like chessmen as tall as houses; roughly squared columns, mighty domes, and boulders like headless birds, spreading huge wings for a flight that is never taken; sheer walls of sandstone eaten into holes and niches till they look like mountains of petrified sponge; rocks that are gray, rocks that are ruddy as if washed in a perpetual sunset, rocks of tawny or creamy yellow, belted with orange and dashed with white; and layers upon layers of stratified sandstone.[33]

"The ground is covered with loose, broken rock from which you may pick up curious pieces perforated like honeycombs, crusted with white and yellow crystals, and flecked with every imaginable color; and you may carry home, as a priceless paperweight, a bit of Echo Canyon, painted in pale green and rich ocher red, with a grain of garnet color shot through."[34]

Miriam's appreciation for the territory of Utah was not limited to the landscape. According to an article in the May 2, 1877, edition of the *Desert News*, she enjoyed meeting the women who resided in the "Land of Latter-Day Saints." "Mormon women were different from what I had expected them to be," Miriam told a reporter, "more intelligent, more womanly, and better contented with their lot. They expressed themselves as not preferring polygamy, but looking upon the practice as part of their religion."[35]

From Utah, the Leslies and their band of followers traveled to Nevada. The moonlight ride across the alkali plains ended in the town of Elko in mid-May 1877. Before arriving at the town in the northeast section of the state, Miriam and company had their eyes fixed on the scenery and noticed what looked like "dark cones" sprinkled among the sagebrush, around which small, moving figures could be seen racing after the train.

Drawing of a scenic location on the Frank Leslie transcontinental trip—Monument Rock at the north end of the Great Salt Lake ACCESSIBLE ARCHIVES, INC., 5 GREAT VALLEY PARKWAY, MALVERN, PA 19355, 866-296-1488, FRANK LESLIE'S WEEKLY, ONLINE DATABASE, PICTURE WITH CAPTION, PAGE 257, DECEMBER 22, 1877 ISSUE. HTTP://WWW. ACCESSIBLE-ARCHIVES.COM/

As the cars slowed approaching in the depot, the voice of a young woman called out, "Indians!"[36]

The train hadn't come to a complete stop before the artists in the Leslie group jumped out of the car, sketchbooks in hand. A number of women and children from the Shoshone tribe had left their tepees and were gathering at the depot. The artists captured the scene with pen and ink drawings. Additional sketches were made of the area and its inhabitants during the group's short stay.[37]

"The town of Elko is a considerable one as towns go on the Humboldt Desert," Miriam wrote of the location. "The bright, white-painted hotel and the two or three neat stores and station buildings have a thriving and busy look in the cheerful, early sunlight.[38]

"According to the guidebooks, Elko has a future as a watering place, boasting of six hot and cold mineral springs, one of which is agreeably known as the 'Chicken Soup Spring' and requires only pepper and salt and a willing imagination to make it a perpetual free soup kitchen. A bathhouse is already erected, and a large hotel is to follow which, it is confidently expected, will bring fashion and civilization by the carload into Elko."[39]

The next stop for the Leslie crew was at the junction of the Virginia and Truckee Railroad, the short line that connects the main transcontinental track to the riches of the Comstock silver mines. On May 26, 1877, the travelers reached Carson City, the capital of Nevada. "Carson considers itself a fine, thriving, full-grown town—quite an old established one, having had twenty years' time to improve and beautify itself and to run up its population to three thousand, five hundred souls," Miriam wrote about the municipality.[40]

"It is not fair to look upon—few of these Western centers of young civilization are. It is only a straggling place, set on a flat plain with the glorious, snowy Sierra stretching away north and south. There are the usual broad streets with stone-paved channels of clear, running water on either side in lieu of our muddy gutters of the East; sparse rows of cottonwood trees with smooth, pale yellow bark; square, two-storied houses in a most severely simple style of domestic architecture; planked sidewalks; stores; saloons; long, low railroad buildings and platforms; and a little square enclosure of fresh, thick, green grass, in the midst of which a fountain is playing.[41]

"We leave our car and wander off on a stroll through the streets. They don't invite the pedestrian to a very extended ramble; in ten minutes one could make a brisk circuit of them all. There is the main street, running north and south, with its two goodly stone buildings, the Mint and the Capital, and its straggling show of shops (most of them with open windows and doors and a view inside of the proprietors making ready to open business for the day)."[42]

Leaving Carson City, Miriam and friends traveled to the boomtown of Virginia City. The fifty-mile erratic line of train tracks the Pullman car followed consisted of sweeping, sharp curves and steady upgrades.[43]

"Like a ship in a storm, our great unyielding car goes swinging around jutting promontories and sharp, cape like spurs," Miriam detailed in her journal. "One or two of the more imaginative members of the party avow themselves seasick. Nowhere on the journey have we passed through a wilder and more desolate land than this; nowhere have we found ourselves so completely in the mountains, or felt so shut in and overshadowed by their grandeur.[44]

Interior of a Wagner drawing room and sleeping car where Miriam Leslie and guests congregated on their journey SOCIETY OF CALIFORNIA PIONEERS, LAWRENCE & HOUSEWORTH 1860/1870 1558 INTERIOR OF WAGNERS' DRAWING ROOM AND SLEEPING CAR WM. M. TWEED

"Only two miles from Gold Hill lies the Silver City itself, with its close-packed population impartially distributed above and below the surface. Every man who has handled a silver dollar has heard of the famous Comstock Lode and is familiar with the names of such bonanza kings as Jones, Sharon, Flood, and O'Brien, whose magnificent wealth has rendered the West famous; but it is doubtful if many persons are as familiar with the aspect of this unique city that is the home of our silver wealth.[45]

"In this first glance the whole aspect of the city is one of intense shabbiness and instability; the low frame houses strike one as only elaborate tents hastily thrown together to meet a temporary need. The sound of the place concentrates, not around the homes, but about these long, low sheds, these smokestacks and flumes, this network of crossing and recrossing railroad switches, these great, gray mounds of crushed quartz—signs of a tremendous labor that never rests, never stops for breathing space, never for one moment relaxes its grip upon the men who are its tools. The mines and shafts are the city; the houses are the accessories."[46]

It was a wet, chilly afternoon when Miriam and friends left Virginia City bound for the Sacramento Valley. In early June, the sojourners' train arrived in Sacramento. The vehicle stopped under a long, covered passage-way lined with refreshment booths and lunch counters and crowded with people. Miriam and the others exited their car and flagged down a pair of horse-drawn carriages to take them through town.[47]

"In less than five minutes we are rattling over an uneven pavement, through a blaze of semitropical sunshine and a cloud of dust, up K Street," Miriam recalled. "Shall we ever forget that half hour in Sacramento? Under that blue mid-summer sky, in that clear atmosphere and soft, bracing, flower-scented air, it seems to us the very most delectable spot that man might ever call home. It looks so quaint and foreign, with its low, wide buildings and wooden arcades, its great, broad, sunny streets, planked sidewalks, and white and yellow adobe houses, each half-buried in its lovely, crowded garden.[48]

"Oh, there never were such homes and such gardens as we see in Sacramento! Every street down which we whirl is shadier and prettier and more picturesque than the last; every cottage, just a little more enticing to eyes that have looked at the bare Plains and the savage mountain passes for so many days."[49]

San Francisco was the next city on the cross-country trek. When the Leslie troupe disembarked, the sky overhead was gray and a strong wind was blowing clouds of dust. Hackmen, carriage drivers, newsboys, and vendors were competing for the attention of potential customers. Miriam and the others took a carriage to the Palace Hotel, where they would be staying for a couple of days. "It was not without a thrill of joy that we welcome the prospect of clean linens, a bath, and a luxurious hotel apartment," Miriam later recalled.[50]

After the Leslie party had a chance to rest and freshen up, they emerged from their rooms ready to explore the city. "The climate of San Francisco seems a point as difficult to settle as the standard of feminine beauty or the intrinsic value of Wagner's music," Miriam shared in her journal. "Everyone agrees that it is exhilarating, that the air is highly charged with ozone, that the brain-worker can accomplish more here than anywhere else, and wear himself out faster. But this ozone is borne upon high, cold winds, alternating with fogs and dampness fatal to any rheumatic or neuralgic tendencies and unfavorable to pulmonary complaints.[51]

"To live in lodgings and to eat in a restaurant in the city is as San Franciscan as much as it is Parisian, and even families possessing houses and domestic conveniences are often to be found at one of these establishments, dining or lunching, just for variety and also, perhaps to see and to be seen.[52]

"A fashionable restaurant for gentlemen is 'The Poodle Dog;' 'Campi's' is as Italian as Naples; and the 'Maison Doree' is Delmonican in every respect. The code of social law in San Francisco permits young ladies to visit these establishments, even at the risk of occasionally encountering a male acquaintance.[53]

"On the whole, we would not advise the widowed mother of a family of lads and lassies to carry them to San Francisco for social training. Although there is a large class of charming, unexceptional, and rigidly moral society, there are several other classes shading into it by almost imperceptible degrees. The bygone days, when every man was a law unto himself, have left their impress in the form of a certain recklessness and willfulness pervading every circle."[54]

The California extravaganza for the Leslies and their traveling companions would not have been complete without a tour of Yosemite. The sight that first moved Miriam was of a great white gleaming structure reaching to the clouds with a streak of bright water flashing down the side. "El Capitan is not a peak or a summit," Miriam remarked in her journal, "it can hardly be called a mountain, but rather, as we have called it, a wall, two miles in length, 3,300 feet in height, white as ivory and of a grandeur, majesty, and power of expression inconceivable to one who has not seen and felt its influence. To know the Yosemite, to see El Capitan, to get a picture into your mind which will be a lifelong delight to yourself, but utterly 'not transferable,' you must do just what we did, go yourself and bring it away.[55]

"Next to El Capitan, we were most impressed, as we drove on through the valley, with the South Dome, or, as the Indians called it, Tis-oa-ack, the Goddess of the Valley, a great shining silvery dome, as perfect as if one cut a globe through with a knife. A little patch of snow rested upon its summit and glittered in the sunshine, and at its edge one tiny shrub, as it looked, which our guide told us was a pine tree of goodly size, as seen through a telescope, for no one has as yet been able to reach the summit of this mountain, the dome itself being tiled as it were with great, smooth, overlapping slabs of granite, curving at an angle of about sixty degrees, and impossible of passage to any natural appliances except wings. No doubt the craving curiosity and love of dominion inherent in man will impel somebody before long to drag all sorts of tools and laborers up the miles of precipice to the foot of this dome and construct some means of ascent, but for the present it lies beyond his grasp, and, if we had our way, should never be invaded."[56]

The Leslies and company began their homeward journey in early June 1877. They arrived safely in New York on June 7, 1877. The total cost for the transcontinental jaunt was fifteen thousand dollars. Miriam penned a book about the venture titled *California: A Pleasure Trip from Gotham to the Golden Gate*. In addition to the descriptions of the pleasure trip from New York to San Francisco, the volume included numerous illustrations. One of the stories included in the book is about the gracious life to be had in a Palace car. The testimonial was written as a rebuttal to those who insisted train travel was monotonous and uncomfortable.[57]

"This is the reality of train travel," Miriam explains in her book. "Look through my glasses—not couleur de rose, I assure you—and take twenty-four hours on the Pullman hotel car as a fair sample of the rest. Peep in at us by lamplight, when the porter is majestically working his way between the berths, making them up in strict rotation, regardless of the prayers of sleepy wretches whose numbers come last in his list.[58]

"The porter is a severe autocrat who patronizes the women and condescends to be playful with the men. His daily life is passed in struggles to suppress our light baggage and keep track of lost penknives, sketchbooks, gloves, and purses. Berth after berth is spread with fresh, clean sheets and heavy rugs, piled with little square pillows, and duly shut in with voluminous curtains; while under each are stowed the occupants' belongings—the satchel, the half-cut magazine that is never read, the portfolio and sketchbooks, a pair of slippers, or a whiskbroom.[59]

"We are divided by a curtain across the aisle: we women, each rejoicing in a whole section all to herself, at one end; and at the other, the turbulent masculine element, 'doubled up,' so to speak, in upper and lower berths and making night gleeful in their own peculiar fashion.[60]

"And do you sleep? The springy roll of the cars, the slight monotonous rocking of your easy, roomy bed, and the steady roar and rattle of the train lull you into dreamland as a child is rocked by his nurse's lullaby. . . . Then the waking—perhaps with a flash of new-risen sunshine across your pillows, or only the first scarlet streak of dawn above the tawny divides. You draw the blankets and rugs closer round your shoulders, for it is chilly, and pushing the pillows higher, you lie staring out for the next hour or two upon the shifting wonder of the great Plains."[61]

Miriam Leslie's book, *California: A Pleasure Trip from Gotham to the Golden Gate,* was a popular seller and received excellent reviews. For those who could afford it, cross-country trips by rail increased.[62]

Ironically, the trip west and back again left the Leslies in debt. Miriam and Frank struggled financially until Frank's death in January 1880. Miriam inherited all her husband's bills, property, and businesses—including his illustrated newspaper. She proved to be an extraordinary businesswoman, paying off all of Frank's creditors and transforming the newspaper into a financial success within five years of Frank's death.[63]

Miriam penned six books and more than fifty articles in her lifetime. The book about her railroad journey across the country was the most popular of all her titles.[64]

CHAPTER 8

Women vs. the Railroad: The Fight for Fairness on the Rails

THE CREATION OF THE RAILROAD SYSTEM IN THE UNITED STATES IS A stirring story of American initiative and enterprise. Every conceivable obstacle stood in the way of the railroad's success. An apathetic public jeered at early efforts to provide rail transportation; it was difficult to convince them that it was safe or profitable. Mechanical difficulties ran all the way from finding engines that would run to perfecting rails, wheels, and signals.

In some eastern locations, tracks were torn up by indignant citizens, and in one city they were declared a public nuisance. A famous newspaper issued a warning that "the use of steam with its train of coaches, its 'soft effeminate cushions causing easement to bodies and legs,' would rob passengers of manliness."[1]

The close relation of railroads to all the people was aptly described by railroad historian Agnes C. Laut in an article in the October 24, 1929, edition of the *Daily Republican*. Laut noted that the railways could prosper "only as the communities they service prosper and their empires prosper. The well-being of one is bound up in the well-being of the other; and neither can be hurt without hurting the other."[2]

The first routes where the tracks could be laid were little more than crude trails through thick undergrowth that led west from Boston and New England along the Mohawk Valley to Lake Erie, from Philadelphia and Baltimore across the Appalachians to the Ohio River Valley, and from Virginia and North Carolina to Nashville and Louisville. For more than thirty years, railway tracks were laid without interruption across the country beginning in the late 1820s. By 1850, they crisscrossed many states, totaling more than nine thousand miles of tracks. Men from all walks of life and many ethnic backgrounds, from the Chinese to the Irish, carved out sections in the vast grasslands, dense forests, and rolling mountains.[3] Women contributed to the grand effort in many ways, not the least of which was refining the creation and making it suitable for all who hoped to benefit from the revolutionary mode of transportation. Women also played a part in bringing about an end to a discriminatory tactic employed by railroad companies.

A great deal was accomplished technologically in a relatively short amount of time in the railroad industry. What didn't progress as quickly as the advancement in conveyance was the acceptance of the population regardless of race or ethnic background. The less attractive element of railroad development was the creation of the Jim Crow car. The car was identical in structure to other passenger cars but contained a partition that would separate the races. The section where people of color would sit had no restroom and often no water fountain.[4]

In 1870 and 1881, the practice of segregating ticket buyers was challenged by two women. In early 1870, Mary Jane Chilton boarded a train in St. Louis with her fifteen-year-old daughter and eight-year-old nephew. The trio was bound for Carondelet, an annexed neighborhood in St. Louis, Missouri. With tickets in hand, Mary proceeded to the ladies' car. A brakeman quickly stepped in front of her and blocked her way. The conductor following behind him approved of his actions. Mary was told that the ladies' car was not for women of color and was instructed to find a place to sit in the smokers' car. Men rode in the smokers' car, most of whom smoked and drank while traveling.[5]

Mary didn't like the smell of smoke, and she was fearful of sitting in a car with strange men. She refused to go and sat down on the steps of the ladies' car. There she stayed until the conductor physically moved her onto the train platform in front of a crowd of cheering bystanders. The train proceeded on its way, leaving Mary and her family to walk to their destination.[6]

Mary sued the St. Louis, Iron Mountain and Southern Railroad Company for five thousand dollars. Not surprisingly, the court found in favor of the railroad. The Missouri Supreme Court upheld the ruling and noted the railway companies had the right to make such regulations regarding the color line.[7]

A similar situation occurred to a family attempting to travel from Kentucky to Cincinnati in August 1881. According to the November 29, 1881, edition of the *Courier Journal*, Reverend William H. Gray purchased first-class tickets for himself; his wife, Selena; and their child to travel on the Cincinnati Southern Railroad. They boarded the train, presented their tickets, and proceeded to the first-class coach. A brakeman stopped them and told them to go to the smoking car. The reverend kindly agreed to go along to the smoking car but pleaded with the railroad conductor to allow his wife and child to ride in the ladies' car. The conductor refused, and when pressed for a reason, the reverend was told it was because of his wife's color. Selena refused to make the trip under the terms offered.[8]

Angry and insulted, the Grays filed suit against the railroad. In an article written by Patricia Minter in the April 1985 edition of the *Chicago-Kent Law Review*, Gray v. Cincinnati Southern Railroad Company charged that the plaintiff was unlawfully and forcibly prevented from entering the first-class coach solely because she was a woman of color and as a result was greatly hindered and delayed in her trip and deprived of her lawful rights as a citizen to accommodations substantially equal to those offered other female passengers of her status.[9]

Selena, Reverend Gray, and several other people of color met at a church in Cincinnati on November 28, 1881, to discuss the widespread discrimination practiced by many of the railroad companies. At the indignation meeting, a collection was taken to help Selena pay for her attorney and court costs. Those present also created a list of resolutions to make their position known to railroad executives that the adverse behavior toward people of color would no longer be tolerated. The resolutions read as follows:[10]

Resolved. That we view with indignation the system of outrages perpetrated upon the colored people of Kentucky and other states by the railroads.

95

> *Resolved. That the colored citizens, in mass meetings assembled, do demand first-class fare for colored persons holding first-class tickets.*
>
> *We further demand the railroad companies make no discrimination on account of color. We shall hail with delight a verdict in favor of Mrs. Selena Gray, in the suit now pending in the United States Court and we pledge our influence and means in the prosecution of the suit.*[11]

Selena Gray did have her day in court, and according to the lawsuit, she placed her damages at fifty thousand dollars. The judge hearing the case found in her favor and awarded her one thousand dollars.[12]

Mrs. Belle Smoot didn't fare as well in court as Selina had. Belle had experienced the same treatment at the hands of the brakeman and conductor on the Kentucky Central Railroad in September 1881. She had paid for accommodations in the first-class car and demanded she be given what she paid for when the railroad officials tried to send her to the smoking car. Belle refused go to the smoking car and was thrown off the train. The September 13, 1881, edition of the *Louisville Bulletin* called her treatment "a high-handed outrage." Belle sued the railroad for ten thousand dollars.[13]

Rather than sue the railroad on the common-law grounds of not being given what was paid for, Belle sued for damages under the Civil Rights Act of 1875. The Civil Rights Act "guaranteed African Americans equal treatment in public transportation and public accommodations and service on juries." The law also made it a crime for "anyone to facilitate the denial of such accommodations or services on the basis of color, race, or previous condition of servitude."[14]

When the case came up for hearing in the United States Court at Covington in Kentucky, the counselor who represented the railroad objected to the petition, claiming the United States Court had no jurisdiction in the case because both plaintiff and defendants were residents of the same state. The court agreed that the prohibitions of the Civil Rights Act applied only to state action, not to those individuals such as the conductor or the policy makers of the railroad. The judge offered Belle the opportunity to make an appeal to the Supreme Court.[15]

The decision made in the Smoot case was an important one, as it was the first upon the points presented ever rendered in the United States.

Several years would pass before segregation on trains was abolished, but the stand Mary Chilton, Selena Gray, and Belle Smoot took against racial bigotry brought attention to the immoral and inhumane practice.

CHAPTER 9

Olive Dennis: The Railroad Civil Engineer

By the beginning of the nineteenth century, with independence won and the Indians largely subdued, the great tide of western movement across the North American continent was gaining momentum. One of the first railroad lines to transport people from the East to the West was the Baltimore and Ohio Railroad. Construction on the Baltimore and Ohio Railroad began in July 1828, and the first stretch of rails was completed in 1830. More than ninety years later, the rail line was still carrying passengers to destinations beyond the Missouri River and still establishing itself as a leader in the industry.

In 1920, Baltimore and Ohio Railroad executives made the bold decision to hire a woman in their engineering department. Not only was Olive Dennis the first female professional engineer hired by the Baltimore and Ohio Railroad, but she was also the first female ever to be hired in that field for a major rail line.[1]

Olive was born on November 20, 1885, in Thurlow, Pennsylvania, and at the age of eleven decided to build her own playhouse. As a child growing up in Baltimore, Olive enjoyed working with tools. She frequently borrowed her father's tools to disassemble her mechanical toys. She spent days watching the construction of a new home across the street from where she lived and was convinced she could duplicate the work she saw being done. Using recycled wood from an old shed her father had torn down, Olive designed and built a playhouse complete with windows, shutters, doors, and a full porch with stairs.[2]

Olive excelled scholastically, graduating from Western High School with honors and a scholarship to attend Goucher College. She

Miss Olive Dennis of the B&O Railroad LIBRARY OF CONGRESS

was elected to Phi Beta Kappa there and achieved a bachelor of arts degree. From Goucher she went on to Columbia in New York, where she received a master's degree in mathematics. While teaching school in Wisconsin, she decided to study civil engineering at Cornell University. Olive was only the second woman in the school's history to pursue such a degree.[3]

It was 1920, and the opportunities for women in the civil engineering field were limited, but Olive persevered. In early 1921, Olive met with Daniel Willard, president of the Baltimore and Ohio Railroad. Willard was impressed with the way she presented herself and hired her to work as a draftsman to design bridges. Olive's presence in a male-dominated field was the subject of a feature article in the February 24, 1921, edition of the *Evening Sun*. "Being a woman practicing a profession in which there are few women is both an advantage and a disadvantage," Olive shared with the *Evening Sun* reporter. "It is an advantage in that if your work is good it will be recognized quickly because of your conspicuousness; it is, however, a distinct disadvantage in obtaining employment. I think one counter balances the other."[4]

Olive responded to the newspaper reporter's questions from her office at the Baltimore and Ohio Railroad offices in Baltimore on Madison Avenue. "But how did you chance to choose civil engineering as a profession?" the journalist queried. "Women aren't supposed to have mathematical minds, you know." Olive smiled politely at the reporter from behind a big, flat-topped drafting board, its surface liberally endowed with paraphernalia of her profession. "It is all a matter of likes and dislikes," she replied. "I have always liked mathematics, and what one likes best, one can do best generally."[5]

The *Evening Sun* reporter described Olive as dainty and slender and noted that she was required to carry a transit with a heavy tripod in the field most days—a feat that fatigued most men. Olive didn't complain about the strenuous duty. It was part of the job, and she was grateful for the opportunity.[6]

"I came here in September," Olive volunteered about the job. "I had tried for any number of positions, but being without experience and being a woman, too, proved too much—especially being a woman, so I had a hard time finding a place." Intrigued, the reporter asked her what plans she had for the future.[7]

"My interest is in the technical part of the profession," Olive shared. "I don't care for the business part. I find that men respect women in new fields, although, of course, there is some prejudice in getting in."[8]

In 1922, Willard called her out of the draftsman pool to take on another assignment, one he hoped would lead to an increase in ticket buyers on the Baltimore and Ohio. Olive was tasked with engineering an upgrade of the interior of the trains that would give passengers a more pleasant and comfortable ride. She took her new position as engineer of services seriously and embarked on several trips with the railroad to learn what improvements were necessary.[9]

During Olive's first year in her new position, she traveled more than forty thousand miles. By riding the train and speaking with her fellow sojourners, she learned firsthand what needed to be done to refine railcars. One of the first things she discovered about passenger service was that the seats in the coaches were so high that the average woman's feet couldn't comfortably reach the floor. The other issue with the seats involved the shape. The Baltimore and Ohio Railroad seats were bench seats. Olive created a new design for an individual seat that would sit lower to the floor and include a shaped back curve that fit into the seat cushion and partially reclined. She was mindful of the role color and fabric type played in creating a pleasing and restful environment, too. Olive redesigned the seats and made sure the color and material used were soothing, plush, and stain-resistant.[10]

Olive's suggestions were submitted directly to the railroad president. In addition to revamping the seats, she proposed larger dressing rooms supplied with free paper towels, liquid soap, and drinking cups for women. Towels, soap, and cups would be provided in men's washrooms as well. Olive also made innovations with the lighting. Ceiling lights above the seats were exceptionally glaring and bright, making it difficult for passengers to see properly or sleep comfortably. Olive designed lights with dimmers.[11]

Another area she improved involved the circulation of air on the passenger cars. She invented an individual window vent that would allow riders to bring in fresh air while trapping dust. Olive held a patent on the ventilator she designed, which stabilized temperatures and kept cinders out without blocking the scenery. Other rail companies introduced similar ventilation systems in the years following the upgrade to the Baltimore and Ohio Railroad cars.[12]

Baltimore and Ohio Railroad executives praised Olive's designs and credited the lady engineer with taking the pain out of the train. Her improvements contributed to the rise in women passengers on the rail line.[13]

In the mid-1940s, Olive helped design a state-of-the-art luxury passenger train called the Cincinnatian. "The new streamliner provides an unusual amount of space per passenger for dining, recreation, and comfort," an article in the January 10, 1947, edition of the *Newark Advocate* read. "Of the total of five cars, only three have seats to be reserved for revenue passengers. The other two, the combination buffet-lounge at the head end of the train and the combination dinner-observation car at the rear, are for the use of all passengers."[14]

The postwar, streamlined train with three coaches, a club car, and an observation diner went into service in January 1947. The one-hundred-foot train ran from Baltimore to Cincinnati and back. Passengers in all the cars had clear, unobstructed views of the picturesque route through the Potomac River Valley. The windows on all the cars were designed to prevent fogging.[15]

Olive Dennis's Cincinnatian was the first postwar train to be placed into service by any eastern railroad and the first to serve the nation's capital.[16]

Not all of Olive's innovations were as grand as the Cincinnatian, but they did make a difference for the average passenger. Olive considered everything about the configuration of the Baltimore and Ohio trains, from the way doors were placed to the items served at the evening meals, and even the dishes in which the food was served. In 1925, Olive created special china to commemorate the 100th anniversary of the Baltimore and Ohio Railroad. She used multiple shades of blue for the trim on a white base background. Various scenic locations and historic locomotives decorated the china pieces. The centenary china took two years to design, and Olive was issued a patent for her work on May 31, 1927.[17]

Centenary china was extremely popular with travelers and was made available to the public to buy. The sale of the pieces was discontinued during World War II because the Baltimore and Ohio Railroad could not obtain new china stock due to rationing.[18]

After thirty years of service, Olive Dennis retired from the Baltimore and Ohio Railroad in 1951. In addition to her work for the rail line, she was a consultant for the Office of Defense Transportation during World War II and the first woman member of the American Railway Engineering Association.[19]

Olive passed away on November 5, 1957, at the age of seventy-two.[20]

CHAPTER 10

Phoebe Snow: The Railroad Pinup Girl

PHOEBE SNOW MIGHT HAVE BEEN A FICTIONAL CHARACTER CREATED BY executive Earnest Elmo Calkins for the Calkins and Holden Advertising Agency in 1900, but she was one of the most influential women in the area of railroad travel for more than twenty years.[1]

Phoebe Snow was created to sell the idea of cleanliness in traveling on a railroad, specifically the Lackawanna, a short line that ran between Buffalo and New York City. The Lackawanna used sootless anthracite coal exclusively for locomotive fuel. Phoebe always wore a spotless white dress that was always cool-looking, comfortable, and corsaged with orchids. She became so popular as a symbol of cleanliness and was lodged so surely in the hearts and minds of train travelers that her name was printed in big, bold, white letters on every piece of equipment owned by the Lackawanna.[2]

Sometime prior to World War I, the Lackawanna decided to introduce a fast, new passenger train to compete in the luxury market for wealthy rail travelers. This new train was to be the last word in elegance, comfort, prestige, and speed. When it came time to find a name, it seemed as if the "Phoebe Snow" was the only name that was considered—yet up to this time, no train had been named for a woman. From that day forward, Phoebe Snow was to become the most famous of all deluxe passenger trains.[3]

In the history of railroading, there were only two other passenger trains that were comparable in elegance, grandeur, and speed to the Phoebe Snow. They were the New York Central's Twentieth Century Limited and the Great Northern's Empire Builder.[4]

Beautiful and always spotless in her white hat, dress, and gloves, Phoebe Snow demonstrates another new feature of the Lackawanna Railroad.

AUTHOR'S COLLECTION

Phoebe Snow ad promoting the Lackawanna Shortline AUTHOR'S COLLECTION

The real Phoebe Snow was the first of all pinup girls, and she was the rage of her day. She was the figment of the imagination of Earnest Elmo Calkins and was first painted by Harry Stacy Benton. The model was Marian Murray Gorsch, one of the first models used in advertising.[5]

Many of the advertisements featuring Phoebe Snow included a short poem. The poem associated with the first advertisement read as follows: "Says Phoebe Snow, about to go upon a trip to Buffalo. My gown stays white from morn till night upon the Road of Anthracite."[6]

Phoebe's career ended in 1922, four years after the end of World War I. Anthracite was needed solely for military use and was subsequently prohibited for railroad use. Phoebe's services were no longer needed.[7]

CHAPTER 11

Julia Bulette:
The Madam Honored by the Railroad

THE COLD, GRAY JANUARY SKY ABOVE VIRGINIA CITY, NEVADA, IN 1867 unleashed a torrent of sleet on a slow-moving funeral procession traveling along the main thoroughfare of town. Several members of the volunteer fire department, Virginia Engine Company Number One, were first in a long line of mourners following a horse-drawn carriage transporting the body of soiled dove Julia Bulette. Playing "The Girl I Left Behind Me," the Nevada militia band shuffled behind the hearse. Black wreaths and streamers hung from the balconies of the buildings along the route that the remains of the beloved thirty-five-year-old woman were escorted. Miners who knew Julia wept openly. Out of respect for the deceased woman, all the saloons were closed. Plummeting temperatures and icy winds eventually drove most funeral-goers inside their homes and businesses before Julia was lowered into the ground.[1]

Julia Bulette was murdered on January 19, 1867, at 11:30 p.m. in her home on North D Street in Virginia City. The fair but frail prostitute told her neighbor and best friend Gertrude Holmes she was expecting company but did not specify who the company might be. Twelve hours later Gertrude discovered Julia's lifeless body in bed. She had been beaten and strangled. Gertrude told authorities that Julia was lying in the center of the bed with the blankets pulled over her head and that the sheets under her frame were smooth. She told police that it appeared as though no one had ever been in the bed with Julia.[2]

Virginia City, Nevada's Julia Bulette NEVADA HISTORICAL COLLECTIONS, BIO_B0290
JULIA BULETTE

The authorities believed the scene had been staged. Marks on Julia's body and tears on the pillow used to smother her indicated she struggled with her attacker. The murderer then set the room to look as though nothing was out of the ordinary. He covered Julia's body in such a way that, at a passing glance, she would merely appear to be asleep. It had fooled the handyman she had employed to come in and build a fire for her each day. When the gentleman entered Julia's home at 11:00 a.m., he believed she was sleeping. He explained to law enforcement officers that he was quiet as he went about his work and left when the job was done. A search of the modest home Julia rented revealed that many of her possessions were missing. The citizens of Virginia City were outraged by the crime.[3]

Julia Bulette was born in London, England, in 1832. She arrived in Virginia City, Nevada, in 1863. Men in the bustling silver mining community supported a number of sporting women, and Julia was no exception. She was an independent contractor. She did not work as a madam of a house of ill repute managing other women in the trade. She had a number of regular customers including Thomas Peasley. Peasley owned a local saloon and was known to be Julia's favorite paramour. In addition to running a business, Peasley was a volunteer firefighter. Julia's interest in the Virginia Engine Company Number One began with him. She supported them monetarily when she could and cheered them on whenever they were called to a job. In recognition of her service, she was presented with a handsome feminine rendition of a fireman's uniform. It consisted of a fireman's shield, front shirt, belt, and helmet embossed with the insignia of Virginia Engine Company Number One. Julia was the only woman who was an honorary member of the volunteer force.[4]

Virginia City police conducted an intense search for Julia's murderer, but four months after her body had been discovered, authorities still had no leads. It appeared as though the unknown assailant had fled the area, and any hope of ever finding the perpetrator had ended. According to the November 9, 1955, edition of the *Reno Gazette*, it wasn't until Mrs. Cazentre, wife of the owner of a small restaurant in Gold Hill, Nevada, stumbled upon a clue to the crime that the police investigation turned around.[5]

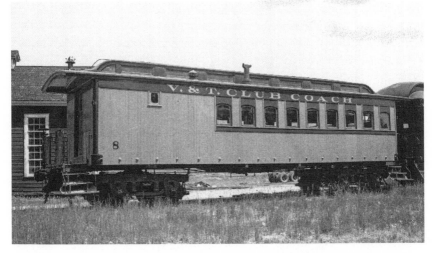

The V&T Railroad Club Coach, also known as the Julia Bulette car
AUTHOR'S COLLECTION

In April 1867, Mrs. Cazentre was looking over a fine piece of silk she was going to use to make a dress when two customers came into the restaurant for breakfast, sat down at a table, and began talking. Their discussion centered on Julia Bulette's brutal murder and the failure of the authorities to find her killer. Mrs. Cazentre overheard the customers mention that the murderer was believed to have stolen two pieces of silk dress material from his victim. Mrs. Cazentre was astonished. A few months prior to this occasion, she had purchased material from a drifter for an incredibly modest price. When she bought the fabric, Mrs. Cazentre asked the salesman how he came to have such a fine piece of material, and the man told her it had once belonged to a lady whose husband had been killed in a mining accident.[6]

After Mrs. Cazentre finished speaking with the two customers, she hurried from the restaurant to the courthouse with the material in tow. She shared everything that had transpired with Judge Jesse S. Pitzer. He then summoned Harry and Sam Rosner, owners of a local mercantile called Rosner and Company, who identified Mrs. Cazentre's silk as the material sold to Julia Bulette. Judge Pitzer then suggested that Mrs. Cazentre view all the drifters, vagabonds, and thugs currently in jail for vagrancy to see if the man who sold her the silk might be among them. It turned out the salesman was indeed incarcerated at the city jail, and Mrs. Cazentre quickly identified him.[7]

The culprit was a Frenchman named John Millian who had been employed at a bakery in town. In March 1867, Millian had attempted to attack one of Julia Bulette's neighbors. He had broken into the neighbor's home carrying a knife. When the woman screamed, he had run. The neighbor had reported the attack to the police and led them through Virginia City in search of Millian. He had been arrested trying to leave town. After Mrs. Cazentre identified Millian within his jail cell, authorities examined a trunk Millian's employer said belonged to him that was stored at the bakery. The trunk was full of Julia Bulette's possessions. Once he was presented with the evidence against him, Millian confessed to the crime.[8]

Charles Dlong, a Virginia City attorney and one-time California state assemblyman, represented Millian. He argued that his client did not murder Julia. He claimed she was killed by two other men and that Millian was asked to store the possessions for them. Millian told the court he did not know the names of the actual killers and could not produce witnesses to support his claim. The case was handed over to the jury eight hours after opening statements had been made. They found Millian guilty of murder, and he was hanged on April 24, 1868.[9]

In October 1945, more than seventy-eight years after Julia Bulette's death, executives at the Virginia & Truckee Railroad in Virginia City paid homage to the slain soiled dove by naming a passenger car after her. The Construction Car No. 8, built in 1869, was the line's first passenger car. It was in service for a brief two years before the car was purchased by MGM Studios. The Julia Bulette car was used in several feature films and television shows. Julia and the railroad car were the subject of a 1959 *Bonanza* episode in which Little Joe falls in love with the infamous courtesan.[10]

CHAPTER 12

Mary Colter: The Harvey House Architect

THE SUN BLAZED HIGH IN A BRASSY SKY, AND HEAT DANCED IN UNDU-lating waves across the high plateau town of Winslow, Arizona. In the far distance, a train with the name Santa Fe Railway embossed on its side hurried along steel rails toward the La Posada Hotel. It was May 15, 1930, opening day for the newest link in the chain of Fred Harvey hotels found along the Santa Fe line between Chicago and the Pacific Coast.[1]

The main lobby of the grand establishment was crowded with local and state politicians, Native Americans, businessmen and their wives, enthusiastic patrons, and of course Harvey Girls, those dedicated women who worked as waitstaff at restaurants and hotels from Kansas to California. Among those celebrating the launch of La Posada was its architect, Mary Colter. The sixty-two-year-old designer beamed with pride as she surveyed the rambling earth-tinted structure. Inspired by the great ranchos of old Mexico, the hotel was the embodiment of simplicity, spacious comfort, and colorful interest, characteristic of early Spanish craftmanship.[2]

One of Mary's friends handed her a glass of champagne to toast the event, but before she could raise her glass, a pair of rowdy, well-dressed cowboys on horseback burst into the entrance of the magnificent vestibule. One of the exuberant men rode over to Mary, hopped off his horse, scooped her up in his arms, and placed her on the check-in counter. The two cowboys celebrated Mary's accomplishment by firing their guns into the air. Before the gathering had a chance to fully process the actions of the joyful pair, the cowboys quickly walked their horses out of the hotel.[3]

Renowned architect Mary Colter LIBRARY OF CONGRESS

Mary Elizabeth Jane Colter's business relationship with Fred Harvey, the hotelier, restaurateur, and retailer, and the Santa Fe Railway lasted more than forty years. The gifted architect and designer created numerous large-scale projects for the Harvey Company and the rail line, all of which helped promote both businesses and made train travel pleasurable for those heading west.[4]

Mary was born on April 4, 1869, in Pittsburgh, Pennsylvania, and from an early age demonstrated an artistic talent. She relocated to St. Paul, Minnesota, with her parents in 1880 and graduated from high school in 1883 at fourteen. Mary's father passed away in 1886, and shortly afterward she moved to San Francisco to attend the California School of Design. Her chief interest was arts and crafts, an artistic movement that emerged during the late Victorian period. It was an art form characterized by hand-craftmanship, native materials, honest construction, and clean, simple designs.

Mary had first become interested in arts and crafts when she was eleven and a relative gave her family a half dozen drawings made by a Sioux Indian. The drawings depicted the 1876 Battle of Little Bighorn.[5] Not only did those drawings influence Mary artistically, but they sparked a lifelong interest in Southwest Indian tribes.[6]

Once Mary graduated from the California School of Design, she returned to Minnesota to help care for her mother and young sister. She took a teaching position at the Mechanic Arts High School in St. Paul. When Mary wasn't helping students develop their own creative styles, she continued with her own studies in design, archaeology, world history, and architecture. She became a much-sought-after artist in the Twin Cities area, designing displays for the armory building in St. Paul, crafting metal dishes, and making jewelry.[7]

A chance meeting with Minnie Harvey Huckel in early 1902 changed Mary's life forever. Minnie was a collector of Southwestern art with aspirations of having her father, Fred Harvey, display and sell Native American art from the Southwest in the gift stores in his hotels. Mary and Minnie had a great deal in common and became fast friends. Minnie admired Mary's work and in a short time persuaded the executives at the Fred Harvey Company to hire the rising designer and architect star.

Railroad passengers inspecting Indian wares in front of the Alvarada's Indian and Mexican Building, designed by Mary Colter LIBRARY OF CONGRESS

The thriving corporation needed a decorator who had an imagination and was familiar with Indian arts and crafts. Mary was well-suited for the position.[8]

Fred Harvey opened his first restaurant for the Santa Fe Railway in 1876. Before Mary was hired, he had spent twenty-five years adding to his chain of eateries along the railways. His contract with the rail line included the development of hotels on the routes and exclusive rights to its dining car service. The Fred Harvey Company was a growing concern, and someone with Mary's talent was essential if the organization was to advance further.[9]

Mary's first assignment for the Harvey Company was to furnish and decorate the Indian and Mexican Building and Museum in Albuquerque, located in the center of what newspapers in 1902 referred to as "the finest hotel in the Southwest." According to the May 10, 1902, edition of the *Albuquerque Citizen*, the massive structure included the Santa Fe Railway depot on one side and the hotel called the Alvarado on the other. Built at a cost of $125,000, the main building was 300 feet long and 190 feet wide, with open court and peristyle. "An Arcade 200 feet long connects

Mary Colter drew on the characteristics of a number of Indian ruins when she designed the watch tower at Desert View. LIBRARY OF CONGRESS

the hotel with the new Santa Fe passenger depot, an edifice which is in perfect harmony with the artistic lines of the Alvarado," the article noted. "The central building is three stories high, with wings and annexes of two stories, and wide verandas. The walls are plastered with a cement of drab color, in pleasing contrast to the red tile roof."[10]

The museum was one of the first things passengers saw while disembarking from the train. The Southwestern Indian artifacts Mary used to decorate the shelves and tables included handwoven rugs, clay pottery, baskets with intricate patterns, and beadwork featuring designs of the Zuni god of war. The pieces she selected to display and how she placed them about the rooms told a story of the artifacts' makers and creativity. Santa Fe Railway ticket holders delighted in examining the profusion of wares to be purchased.[11]

Executives at the Harvey Company and the Santa Fe Railway were thrilled with the job Mary did. The way she had grouped items together

An example of Mary Colter's exceptional interior design talent in the dining room at La Fonda Hotel in Santa Fe, New Mexico LIBRARY OF CONGRESS

to inspire buyers to decorate their homes using the artwork exhibited and demonstrated a sense of salesmanship the business owners appreciated. Mary wasn't simply an artist, she understood commerce as well.[12]

In 1904, Mary began work on a second project for the Harvey Company and the Santa Fe Railway. Looking to capitalize on the growing tourist attraction that was the Grand Canyon, the two firms decided to build a market for Native American crafts on the south rim of the natural wonder. Plans to construct a train depot and hotel in the area were being made as well. Mary was tasked with designing a structure that would acknowledge the influence of the Indians of the Southwest and act in harmony with the setting. She took her inspiration from the Hopi Indian dwellings—multistoried homes made from mud, native stone, and local timbers for ceiling beams. According to the biography about Mary titled *Mary Colter: Architect of the Southwest* by Arnold Berke, the architect "reproduced the size, proportions, and materials using local Kaibab limestone for the structure, Coconino sandstone for the facing, and peeled, local logs for the floor and roof supports, although she relied on sections of Santa Fe rails to span some of the wider openings."[13]

Finished on New Year's Day 1905, the three-story building was reddish in color, with mesquite pinyon wood ladders that provided access to the terraces on each level. Mary's attention to detail made certain the interior of the pueblo was as genuine as the exterior. The corner fireplaces and chimneys were made from broken pottery jars stacked and mortared together, and vigas were installed on the ceiling and thatched with young trees.[14]

Mary decorated the Hopi House with Kachina dolls, baskets, wood carvings, pottery, jewelry, and handwoven Navajo blankets and rugs. Apart from the main area of the structure where the majority of the goods for sale were housed, Mary set aside rooms to display artwork of the Northwest Coastal Indians and artifacts of the Spanish-Mexican culture.[15]

When the Hopi House officially opened for business, customers enjoyed a unique shopping experience. In addition to being able to browse through one-of-a-kind arts and crafts, they got to see the Native artisans at work. Whether weaving rugs or baskets, Hopi Indians were on-site to share with consumers the skill and creativity that went into each piece made.[16]

In 1910, Mary took a permanent position with the Harvey Company and relocated to Kansas City, Missouri, where the corporate offices were located. She frequently traveled cross-country via the Santa Fe Railway to visit Fred Harvey restaurants and hotels. One of the trips she took was to the town of Lamy, New Mexico, south of Santa Fe. Lamy was an important location for the railroad as it was the junction between the railroad's main east-west line and Santa Fe. It was determined that a hotel needed to be built at the location to service train passengers and railroad crews who worked in the area maintaining the passage. The hotel was called the El Ortiz, and Mary's job was to decorate the interior.[17]

The palatial hotel was a one-story affair with ten guest rooms that opened onto an enclosed patio where an elaborate fountain could be

The Hopi House at the Grand Canyon National Park, one of several buildings in the park designed by Mary Coulter LIBRARY OF CONGRESS

seen. Once again Mary used a mixture of Mexican and Native influences to create an aesthetically pleasing look. Using sections of old telephone poles, she constructed vigas for the ceilings and planter boxes. As in her other designs, Navajo rugs, beaded wall hangings, and Mexican colonial benches, bowls, trays, and clay jars decorated the interior. The main foyer of the hotel featured a large fireplace with patterned brick work. Thick, dark wooden tables and chairs, some with leather backs, perched on top of colorful Native rugs, filled the inviting room. The light fixtures and sconces Mary designed were rustic and made with Southwestern textiles.[18]

The El Ortiz was celebrated by executives at the Harvey Company and the Santa Fe Railway as "the gem of the rail line." According to the July 24, 1911, edition of the *Arizona Republic*, visitors were routinely surprised to find such a beautiful establishment in such a remote location. "There is no other feature of the Santa Fe that has so served to make the line popular as has the chain of perfectly equipped restaurants and hotels created along the route from Chicago to the Pacific Coast," the article elaborated. "Like an oasis in the desert, the dining and lunchrooms have been placed where they are most available and convenient to the traveling public.[19]

"So careful have been the managers of the system in placing these houses at the point where they are most needed that there is at present

The Lobby of the El Ortiz, Fred Harvey Inn at Lamy, New Mexico, designed and decorated by Mary Colter LIBRARY OF CONGRESS

not a single city or junction point of importance along the entire line of the Santa Fe where the sign 'Fred Harvey' does not appear before a dining or lunch room. . . . [20]

"No description is adequate to the taste used in the construction of the Harvey hotels, and the excitement of travelers alighting tired and travel worn, to find themselves before a hotel capable of giving a service not surpassed in the country's largest cities, furnish the most eloquent and convincing praise of the architect, the builder, and above all, of Harvey himself, who had the foresight to realize the need of such a system, and the initiative and ability to perfect it.[21]

"Traveling over the line of the Santa Fe a few days ago, the worker found himself held over at Lamy, a junction point on the main line. Three hours of waiting were staring him in the face and a drizzling rain outdoors made the prospect a little worse than dismal. On sight of a Harvey house with a peculiar sign before it marked 'El Ortiz' he picked up courage to believe that the evening might be pleasant in spite of the murky weather.[22]

"A cold wind had come up with the rain, and the glow of a log fire in the open fire place of the large hotel living room gave a cordial welcome that caused the rain and the hours of waiting to be forgotten.... 'Who would have expected to find such a beautiful room and such a building in this isolated place?' the traveler wondered aloud. As no one had expected it, except those who knew the perfection of the Harvey system by previous experience, there was no replies advanced to this wondering interrogation."[23]

Buffalo Bill Cody appreciated the hotel and Mary's work as well. The January 23, 1911, edition of the *Santa Fe New Mexican* reported on the Wild West showman's stay. "Bill was greatly impressed with the Spanish style of the El Ortiz and after he had viewed the placita and seen the various rooms, he toasted his shins in front of the immense fireplace on which blazed a log that reminded him of the frontier days," the article noted. "The great scout and hunter said with a sign of pleasure, 'Gee, but this would make a cracker jack ranch house, now wouldn't it, boys?' "[24]

After proving herself with three distinctive projects, the powers-that-be at the Harvey Company and the Santa Fe Railway decided to give Mary the monumental task of decorating the restaurants and shops at the Kansas City Union Station. Construction for the magnificent structure began in 1913 and cost seven million dollars. Fourteen railroad lines would use the station, and hundreds of thousands of passengers would visit the train stop. It would be the third-largest train station in the United States, and the principals at the Santa Fe Railway and the Harvey Company wanted the terminus to be beautiful and modern and to provide the best comfort and convenience for travelers.[25]

Designing the Union Station was much grander than Mary's previous assignments. She decided to create a look that ran counter to what she had done before. Instead of oak beams and mantels, she used Roman columns and gold inlay countertops. It was opulent with marble floors and crystal chandeliers. A massive celebration was held on October 30,

1914, to commemorate the grand opening of the station Mary had spent more than a year decorating. "Travelers will be sent on their way in style," an article in the November 6, 1914, edition of the *Atchison Daily Globe* noted about the terminal. "Every convenience has been installed for the service of travelers. Elevators will convey passengers from train sheds to waiting rooms; information booths are conveniently situated in the main lobby; facilities for handling baggage are the most up-to-date. The dining and lunch rooms are under the management of Fred Harvey, and that means perfection in the culinary department."[26]

Shortly after Mary completed the job in Kansas City, she began another project out west. She returned to the Grand Canyon to oversee construction on a building she designed that would be known as Hermit's Rest. The structure would serve as a rest area for tourists disembarking the Santa Fe train and horse-drawn carriages traveling along the trail of the south rim of the canyon. Sightseers could picnic or have afternoon tea at the scenic location.[27]

A suggestion was made early in the planning by an executive at the Harvey Company that Mary design a rest stop that looked like a Swiss chalet. She disregarded that idea and decided to create a hideaway that resembled a place a hermit might build. Mary not only designed the unique building but helped with the construction as well, from the selection of the timber to be used to the placement of every stone. When completed, the structure looked exactly as Mary had hoped—a wobbly pile of boulders and timber ready to tumble into the canyon.[28]

The interior of Hermit's Rest was one large room, forty-six by eighteen feet, with a large fireplace and hardwood floors dotted with the skins of wild animals. Travelers passed through an arch of massive boulders as they made their way to the rest stop. Mary installed an immense bell she found at an antique store in the archway.[29]

Over the years, tourists from all over the world used the setting as a perfect spot to photograph family and friends. The cost to build Hermit's Rest was thirty-nine thousand dollars. Mary's accomplishment was praised by administrators at the railroad, the Harvey Company, and by vacationers to the spot. "Everything around bespeaks the hand and ideas of a genius in design and workmanship," a reporter in the May 29, 1915, edition of the *Ogden Standard* offered about Mary's creation.[30]

Lookout Studio was created as a space where tourists could best view the scenic Grand Canyon and where they could purchase traditional handmade Southwestern and Native American items. Perched on a cliff, Mary designed the building to look as though it was growing out of the surrounding ledges. The structure, built in 1914, was made from Kaibab limestone, had three viewing decks, and a crooked chimney. Mary, who intended Lookout Studio to recall the Anasazi ruins from the Four Corners area, created its ramshackle air by letting weeds grow from the roof. The rough features further allowed the building to blend in with the landscape. Mary's goal with all the construction she did at the Grand Canyon was to make the structures appear not so much built as left behind.[31]

The interior of Lookout Studio was as equally well thought out as the exterior. A rustic, arched, stone fireplace stood in the main room of the building. There were exposed stone walls all around the timber-framed ceilings. The scored concrete floors were decorated with Indian rugs, and photographs of maps of the canyon were scattered about the substantial desks and tables.[32]

A Fred Harvey Santa Fe Railway brochure from 1938 describes Lookout Studio as "severe and contemplative." The brochure recounted, "It's a tiny, rustic club with bright hued Navaho rugs, electric lights, cozy fireplace, and many easy chairs. One may sit through the long, quiet, still days, and rest and read and watch the changes caused by sun and shadow upon the panorama spread below."[33]

Tickets on the Santa Fe Railway increased as news of the Harvey Company's contributions to the Grand Canyon area was promoted. Additional lodging was necessary to accommodate the steady influx of tourists to the Arizona location. Once again Mary was called upon to create such a building. In late 1916, she began designing a collection of cottages to be built at the head of Bright Angel Trail at the south rim of the canyon. The sketches she made for the project were of stone cabins with vigas that protruded above the main and rear entrances. The building of Indian Gardens, as it was tentatively called, was halted in April 1917 when the United States entered World War I. The government appropriated the railways to transport supplies from one area of the country to the other. Train service to the Grand Canyon was halted until the conflict could be resolved.[34]

Mary's services were not needed by the Santa Fe Railway or the Fred Harvey Company for the Grand Canyon area until 1921, when another tourist facility was needed. This time Mary would be working on a project inside the canyon rather than on the rim. She called her design Phantom Ranch. It would be comprised of a main lodge and four two-person cabins. The modest stone-framed buildings would be constructed using material gathered at the location. According to Mary Colter's biography, the wood for the doors and windows had to be hauled to the site by mule. Chimneys for the fireplaces and low-pitched gable roofs were featured on each building. The stained, muted color used to paint the wood and the green used for the roofs were selected because they mingled perfectly with the setting.[35]

The grand opening of Phantom Ranch was held on November 9, 1922. Earlier in the year, a circular about the destination had been issued by the Santa Fe Railway promotional department. The circular encouraged tourists to take the train to the Grand Canyon and hike the trails to the "beautiful" Phantom Ranch. "This unique little ranch, occupying several acres alongside Bright Angel Creek and walled in on two sides by rocks thousands of feet high, is about half a mile beyond the suspension bridge across the Colorado River where Bright Angel Canyon opens into the granite gorge," the Santa Fe Railway advertisement read. "It is the deepest down of any canyon ranch in the world. There's nothing like it anywhere."[36]

Mary's next venture to enhance traveling by rail was the renovation of the Alvarado Hotel in Albuquerque, New Mexico. It was the largest hotel in the Harvey Company chain. The improvements Mary made to the establishment, built in the early 1900s, cost more than a quarter million dollars. The wing she designed to be added onto the existing structure had seventy-six bedrooms, each with a private bath; a barber shop; and an assembly hall seating 250 people. Mary's plan included adding decorative treatments to harmonize with the mission style of the hotel.[37]

According to the January 1, 1922, edition of the *Evening Herald*, Mary was committed to preserving the Spanish atmosphere of the establishment. "On each side of the addition there will be a little Spanish garden surrounded by walls with small gateways and picturesque openings," the *Evening Herald* article explained. "In the garden facing the [rail] road tracks there will be a Spanish fountain lending a charm and color which will delight the traveler.... While the decorations of the public rooms will follow the quaint Spanish style, the bedrooms of the new addition will be modern in every detail.... Throughout the length of the enlarged lobby the Spanish feeling will be strong, with walls and ceiling of rough plaster and wood and furniture of quaint mission design. Lighting will be torches designed from ancient examples of Spanish wrought-iron work."[38]

The renovation of the Alvarado Hotel took six months, and shortly after its completion, Mary traveled to Gallup, New Mexico. Gallup was on the Santa Fe Railway's main line, and executives with the railroad and the Harvey Company believed the hotel and the train station in the fast-growing town needed an overhaul. Mary's assignment was to duplicate the success she'd had improving the Alvarado Hotel with the El Navajo. She was grateful for the opportunity because she could once again draw on her passion for Native American arts and crafts to design a one-of-a-kind structure.[39]

The look Mary used to revitalize the El Navajo was more modern than other structures she designed. The addition, housing a hotel and restaurant, featured sharp edges, a flat roof, unique groupings of windows, and square balconies. The interior of the building mirrored the distinctive exterior with smooth concrete floors and polished ceiling beams. Mary furnished the hotel with thick chairs, wicker settees, Navajo rugs, and Indian pottery and baskets. She added framed Navajo sand paintings to the walls throughout the hotel. The use of the traditional art was celebrated at the official opening of the El Navajo in late May 1923.[40]

"I have just returned from Gallup, New Mexico, the big coal mining town in McKinley County, where I witnessed the ceremonials in the dedication of the new modern hotel called El Navajo, built by the Santa Fe Railway company for the Fred Harvey system," an article in the May 29, 1923, edition of the *El Paso Times* noted about the opening of the El Navajo. "I witnessed the ceremonies performed in the dedication by the chiefs, braves and warriors of the great Navajo Indian nation, the most powerful and prosperous Indians in the United States, who still maintain their ancient customs, rites and ceremonies and are the last of the 'vanishing Americans.'[41]

"The unique feature of the ceremonies was the decoration of the hotel with sand paintings used with the consent and approval of the Indians, through which their religious belief and tribal history are handed down from generation to generation with the understanding that the hotel and sand paintings should be blessed by the Navajo ceremonies, and this is the first time that they ever consented for the presentation of these paintings."[42]

Mary Colter would go on to renovate and expand other Harvey Company hotels along the Santa Fe Railway including the La Fonda in Santa Fe, New Mexico, and the La Posada in Winslow, Arizona. With each lofty assignment, Mary created extraordinary buildings that stood as comfortable works of art for railroad passengers.

One of the last significant structures Mary was asked to design at the Grand Canyon was the Watch Tower. Located on the east rim at Desert View, the Watch Tower would provide sightseers traveling to the canyon via the Santa Fe Railway with another vantage point to enjoy the natural wonder. Mary's inspiration for the design of the observation tower was the Round Tower at Cliff Palace in Mesa Verde National Park. The Cliff Palace in Colorado is the site of the Puebloan cliff dwellings. The Round Tower was built on top of a huge sandstone boulder more than thirteen centuries ago.[43]

After several months studying the Pueblo Indians' construction techniques and the materials used, Mary submitted plans for the building to the Harvey Company in June 1931. The base of the tower was made of steel and set in concrete; layers of stone were then added to the foundation. The stones used were collected from a small canyon near the building site. The position and grouping of the stones, in addition to their size, gave the appearance of being haphazardly placed, something only nature could produce. Mary strived to ensure the buildings she created at the Grand Canyon would not detract from the landscape.[44]

Adjacent to the Watch Tower was a kiva, a subterranean building or room used by Pueblo Indians for religious rites. It wouldn't have been a true Mary Colter architectural design had she not paid homage to the Indians who inspired her work. The interior of the structure was decorated with murals by artist Fred Kabotie. Kabotie, a celebrated Hopi painter and illustrator, filled the kiva with drawings depicting the physical and spiritual origins of Hopi life.[45]

The Harvey Company and the Santa Fe Railway hosted a grand opening commemorating the completion of the Watch Tower on May 13, 1933. Among the hundreds of guests on hand for the event were more than sixty native dancers, drummers, and chanters. The Indians performed a dance to bless the building. During the dance, gifts of apples and oranges were presented and distributed among the Hopi Indian children. According to the May 22, 1933, edition of the *San Bernardino County Sun*, the giving of the fruit was an act of charity to win consideration from the "mighty rain gods."[46]

The other invited guests who came to admire the newly constructed landmark expressed their admiration for the work and the setting. "From the Watch Tower at Desert View, a high point twenty-five miles east of El Tovar hotel and Bright Angel Lodge, you get an extended view of the river which at this point is five miles down, and an exceptionally long-range view of the Canyon, both east and west," one newspaper report at the opening ceremony explained. "From the Watch Tower we could see, in the far distance, the Painted Desert where is located the Hopi and the Navaho Indian reservation. From here you can also trace the course of the Little Colorado, with its seven to one-thousand-foot sheer, granite walls, and note where it joins the Colorado River. It was breathtaking."[47]

Executives at the Santa Fe Railway and the Harvey Company were confident such reports would reach hundreds of individuals and their families looking for a vacation destination. The hope of the two major businesses was to encourage travelers to come west and experience the extraordinary landscapes as well as the Native American lifestyle. For more than twenty years, Mary Colter's contributions helped the companies realize their objective.[48]

CHAPTER 13

Mary Louise Lawser:
The Santa Fe Railroad Muralist

TALENTED PAINTER AND SCULPTOR MARY LOUISE LAWSER ATTENDED college in Pennsylvania and was part of a group comprising several female artists.. They were known as the Philadelphia Ten.[1] Like Mary Colter, Mary Lawser was hired by a major rail line company to help promote westward travel.[2]

Born in 1906 in Pennsylvania, she exhibited a talent for drawing at a young age. She attended the Pennsylvania Museum School, the Pennsylvania Academy of Fine Arts, and the École des Beaux-Arts in Paris. Mary's work was exhibited in galleries in Europe and New York. She was recognized by her peers as a gifted bronze-work artist. After graduation, she took a position as an art instructor at Cedar Crest College in Allentown, Pennsylvania, and at Bryn Mawr.[3]

In early 1940, she was hired to work for notable architect Paul Cret. The French-born, Philadelphia architect and industrial designer was impressed with Mary's design and execution of bronze tablets found inside Alexander Hamilton's home, the Grange. Commissioned by the American and Historic Preservation Society, the tablets were made to honor Alexander Hamilton, first secretary of the United States treasury. In addition to designing buildings on the University of Texas campus and the Pan American Union Building in Washington, DC, Paul Cret designed railroad cars for the Burlington and Santa Fe rail lines. While Mary was employed by Cret, she contributed to decorating various

Mary Lawser's work was a major attraction on the California Zephyr. AUTHOR'S COLLECTION

Mary Lawser painted a number of images for cars on the Santa
Fe Railway. CALIFORNIA STATE RAILROAD MUSEUM LIBRARY

railroad passenger cars with sculptures, wood carving, and mixed-metal creations.[4]

When Cret passed away in 1945, Mary was hired by another respected Pennsylvania architect, John Harbeson, to aid him in creating a new look for Burlington's Pioneer Zephyr. Although in the employ of Harbeson, Mary was singled out by the Budd Company, a railroad industry manufacturer, to design murals for the interior of the passenger cars that would inspire ticket-buyers to go west.[5]

In 1948, Mary began work on a mural for the California Zephyr's Silver Lariat. The train was built as a dome coach, a series of cars that have glass domes on the top where passengers can ride and see in all directions around the train. Mary painted a mural of the Pony Express in the large dining and lounge car.[6]

Over the course of her five-year business relationship with the Budd Company, she created murals for the Atchison, Topeka and Santa Fe; the Denver and Rio Grande Western; and the Western Pacific Railroad. Mary's murals generally adorned the end walls of the dome coaches, and they always depicted Western historical themes. She also sculpted the appliqués of apples and grapes that hung at each end of the dining cars as well as the lyre-based radio speakers.[7]

Mary Lawser died in 1985 at the age of seventy-nine.

CHAPTER 14

The Harvey Girls:
The Railroads' Hospitality Ambassadors

IN 1897, TWENTY-YEAR-OLD MABEL SLOAN OF FLORENCE, KANSAS, responded to an ad in the local paper. Looking for work, she was intrigued by the notice: "Wanted: Young women, 18 to 30 years of age, of good character, attractive and intelligent, as waitress in Harvey Eating Houses in the West. Good wages, with room and means furnished."[1] Despite her mother's objection of "women don't hold jobs outside of the home," Mabel responded to the advertisement and accepted a position as one of entrepreneur Fred Harvey's growing number of counter girls in his restaurants across the country. After a vigorous training period, Mabel was sent to waitress at the Casa del Desierto, House of the Desert, in Barstow, California.[2]

For several months, Mabel served the men and women who traveled through the area on the Atchison, Topeka and Santa Fe Railway. Dressed in her neat, black dress and crisp, starched white apron, she tended to customers' culinary needs and made sure their dining experience lacked for nothing.[3]

Homer Pike, a farmer in his late forties from Hamilton, Montana, was one of the patrons who in early 1898 visited the Harvey House where Mabel was employed. Homer was known among his friends as being frugal. He did his own cooking, washed and mended his own clothes, and refused to buy additional clothing even though the fabric was thin and fading on the garments he owned. It was rumored he had plenty of money but spent little if nothing on frivolity. He showed no interest in women or

Harvey Girls standing in front of the Atchison, Topeka and Santa Fe Railway's Fred Harvey House in Syracuse, Kansas KANSAS STATE HISTORICAL SOCIETY

marriage and spent a great deal of time by himself—that is, until Mabel waited on him at the Casa del Desierto.[4]

According to an article in the May 16, 1899, edition of the *Ravalli Republic*, Horace was smitten with Mabel the moment she brought him a cup of coffee. The two exchanged pleasantries, and after three days, he dared to ask Mabel to take a walk with him. She agreed, and two days later, the pair decided to marry. Mabel resigned from her position with Fred Harvey, relocated to Montana, and lived out the rest of her life with Homer, who showered her with affection and spoiled her with all the things his money could buy.[5]

Not every woman employed as a Harvey Girl found matrimony while on the job, nor did they take on such work with that in mind. The possibilities for the thousands of young women who answered Fred Harvey's call for waitresses were endless. The Harvey Girls were considered the belles of the West, and they left an indelible mark on the history of the Transcontinental Railroad.

Three young Harvey Girls en route to the restaurant where they would be working along the Atchison, Topeka and Santa Fe Railway line KANSAS STATE HISTORICAL SOCIETY

Historians believe the Harvey Girls played a significant role in the taming of the Wild West. They brought culture, refinement, and romance to the frontier where buffalo herds, attacking Indians, and horse thieving were common. The man responsible for the successful movement was an Englishman named Frederick Henry Harvey. Born in London in 1835, Harvey was a businessman who founded a chain of eating houses along the Santa Fe Railway line. He was living in Leavenworth, Kansas, with his wife and children when the opportunity presented itself. Early in Harvey's marriage, Fred co-owned a successful restaurant in St. Louis and served as a pantryman for a small café. His duties included preparing hors d'oeuvres, properly seasoning all appetizers before they were served, and storing food items.[6]

Harvey's association with the railroad began in 1862, when he worked as a mail clerk for the Hannibal and St. Joseph. By 1865, he was employed as a ticket agent for the Burlington line. Later he became a general western freight agent; traveling the rails as a representative of the rail line, Harvey transacted business with individual customers and corporations.[7]

During his time away from home and his wife, Sally, and her exceptional cooking, Harvey recognized the need for good food to be served to passengers making their way from one depot to another. Most often, railroad passengers brought their own box lunches with them on their long journeys and hoped the food would last the entire trip. They used the routine, twenty-minute stops to rush into towns where sometimes only the local saloon offered dining opportunities. Harvey decided he was the one to furnish travelers with those much-needed meals. He began by opening two cafés on the Kansas Pacific Railroad line, one in Wallace, Kansas, and the other in Hugo, Colorado.[8]

The small venture proved to be successful. Harvey then presented an idea for a system of restaurants tied to railroad stops to executives at the Burlington Railroad, but they refused to see the value of his plan. Undeterred, Harvey brought the business opportunity to officials at the Atchison, Topeka and Santa Fe Railway. The rail line executives were enthusiastic about Harvey's proposition and entered into an exclusive contract with him on May 1, 1889. Harvey would manage and operate all

ATTRACTIVE
OPPORTUNITIES
IN HOTEL EMPLOYMENT

are offered to respectable women, experienced and inexperienced, as waitress, lunch counter attendants, maids, pantry women, etc., under advantageous conditions.

GOOD HOMES.
GOOD TREATMENT.
INCREASED WAGES.

with further increases after six months of satisfactory service.

Also need respectable lunch counter waitresses for our restaurant in the city.

FRED HARVEY,

18th-st. and Wentworth-av., Chicago.

A popular ad posted to recruit Harvey Girls AUTHOR'S COLLECTION

the dining and hotel facilities along the Atchison, Topeka and Santa Fe Railway west of the Missouri River.[9]

Passengers traveling the rail line poured into the Harvey Houses along the route. The immaculately kept establishments featured delicious food served with silver and china atop fine Irish linen tablecloths. "Meals by Fred Harvey" meant travelers would be cared for in style. Railroad executives quickly realized an increase in ticket sales and attributed it to the Harvey Houses. Advertisements for the railroad capitalized on the popularity of the Harvey lunch stands and hotel facilities. "Fact 1—the Santa Fe Railroad continues to sell tickets to most points on earth at reduced rates," an advertisement in the March 22, 1890, issue of the *Topeka Daily Capital* noted. "Fact 2—the Santa Fe Route runs elegant, new reclining chair cars on its Denver train, and its eating house service (Fred Harvey's, everybody knows what kind of meal Fred Harvey gets up) is a drawing card."[10]

WANT-AD WONDERS Trade Mark

Want Ads Used to Recruit Famous Fred Harvey Girls

WANTED—Young women of good character, attractive and intelligent, 18 to 30, for...

To staff the famous chain of attractive restaurants he established along the Santa Fe railroad after the Civil War, Fred Harvey used Want Ads. At least 5,000 ranchers and railroad men are estimated to have picked brides from the demure girls Harvey's ads attracted to the romantic frontier life.

Want Ads Are Job-Fillers

$5 to first sender of each true newspaper Classified Advertising result story we accept. Howard Parish, Box 126, NW Br., Miami 47, Fla.

6-29
© 1952 Howard Parish

A popular ad posted to recruit Harvey Girls AUTHOR'S COLLECTION

Harvey was pleased the eateries were so well received, and he was dedicated to upholding the stringent standards he had introduced at his establishments. He routinely visited every one of the Harvey Houses to inspect the food, service, and cleanliness of the dining halls. Early on, Harvey had recognized that the high quality he expected could best be realized by a primarily female staff. Rough, unrefined men residing in remote rail towns could not maintain the expert service required by

THE HARVEY GIRL

Winning hearts in the West...'n East, too, is this newest Lil' Alice inspired by the Fred Harvey girls. Quaint cotton with bonnet sleeve, full skirt and deep yoke ruffle. Junior sizes. $5.95

Thornton's

DEPT. STORE
"A City Within Itself"
4th and Oak

The Harvey Girls were so popular and well respected that clothing designers copied their look to sell to young women across the country. AUTHOR'S COLLECTION

Harvey and expected by his customers. In 1883, he began a broad campaign recruiting women to work for his expanding company.[11]

More than twenty thousand women applied for work at the Harvey Houses across the frontier. The same pioneering spirit that sent restless young men into the West drew the Harvey Girls. Many were schoolteachers lured West by the excitement of the unknown and a chance, perhaps, for romance. They were single and selected from good homes in the East. Once approved, new hires were asked to sign a six- or nine-month contract and agreed to go to whichever Harvey dining hall they were assigned. The girls were housed in dorms presided over by housemothers and had a 10:00 p.m. curfew. They were looked after as carefully as boarding school students at "female seminaries" in the East. The girls were paid $17.50 a month plus board, room, and tips. The uniform of a Harvey Girl resembled that of a nun. They wore plain, starched, black-and-white skirts, bibs, aprons, high-collared shirts, black shoes, and no makeup. Harvey wanted the girls to be as respected as sisters from the church. Harvey Girls had to adhere to the fundamentals set forth by the company: Number one, have a sincere interest in people. Number two, like all your daily contacts with guests. Number three, radiate cheer and make guests feel at ease and at home.[12]

All Harvey Girl recruits began their thirty-day training period in Topeka or Emporia, Kansas, working without pay during that time. The list of duties was extensive, and women had to learn on the job the proper way to serve many customers during the rush of trains stopping at the busy depots. The frantic pace quickly separated the strong, take-charge girls from those who struggled to keep up with the sea of travelers passing through. Those who did well were rewarded for their competency with promotions to head waitress. Harvey Girls who stayed after the contracted obligation were rewarded with silver brooches indicating the length of time they'd been with the company.[13]

The average workday for a Harvey Girl was twelve hours and the average workweek was six days. When the girls weren't serving meals, they were taking care of the dining hall itself: scrubbing floors, cleaning tables, and laundering the fine linens used daily. They also polished the silver and made sure the windows and counters were spotless.[14]

Harvey meals included as many as seven entrees with "seconds and all for seventy-five cents." Menus were coordinated to avoid duplication on a trip. If you had prime rib at one depot stop, you had chicken at another. Those Harvey Girls taking orders for coffee, tea, or milk arranged cups according to a code, and the "drink girl" immediately following served accordingly. The cup's position was the key. Right side up meant coffee, and upside down was hot tea. Upside down and tilted meant iced tea. Upside down and away from the saucer signaled milk.[15]

Passengers had plenty of time to eat their meals. The girls were quick to refill travelers' cups and serve desserts as soon as the meal concluded. Five minutes before the train was ready to get on its way again, a signal was given to alert those lingering over their last delicious bite. Total time allotted for meals was thirty minutes.[16]

According to the book *The Harvey Girls* by Lesley Poling-Kempes, more than 45 percent of the women employed by Harvey were from rural America. These girls were given the opportunity to travel the country and expand their horizons outside the farms and small towns where they were born. During their vacations, the Santa Fe Railway provided them free transportation anywhere along the line. Many of the women who enjoyed venturing into unknown areas in Arizona, New Mexico, California, and Texas eventually decided to settle there, marry, and start a family.[17]

For those women interested in attending college, they found the Harvey Company to be more than accommodating. Their daily schedules were adjusted so they could go to classes. Holding down a full-time job and being a full-time student wasn't an easy task, but many Harvey Girls graduated from the University of New Mexico with degrees that propelled them into careers beyond waitressing.[18]

There were Harvey Girls who took advantage of their respected position and entered beauty contests, competing to win cash and trips to Niagara Falls and Canada. Others made newspaper headlines when they joined forces with bank robbers, fleeing locations where they stole money and soliciting the help of Harvey Girls to get away from the law.[19]

Harvey Girls were strictly forbidden from becoming romantically involved with other Harvey employees. They could not fraternize with the busboys or chefs. If caught, they were immediately dismissed. There were also rules in place for dating customers. It wasn't forbidden, but it was discouraged. Harvey Girls were subjected to unsolicited attention by men from all walks of life. Women were scarce and men plentiful in the West. Some cowboys would eat six or seven times a day just for the pleasure of gazing at the Harvey Girls. Dollar tips were plentiful, and girls received more than twenty requests for dates daily.[20]

According to the August 15, 1948, edition of the *American Weekly*, between 1883 and 1905, 8,260 Harvey Girls were reported to have married railroad men, ranchers, cowboys, and fellow employees—chefs, busboys, clerks, and cooks. Legend has it that by the early 1900s, more than 3,000 babies had been named Fred or Harvey or both. "Fred Harvey offered the first means by which respectable young women could go after the young men who went West," the *American Weekly* article read. "Fred probably did more to tame and civilize the great open spaces than did any other one man—by simple means of turning civilized young women loose in them."[21]

A newspaper account from 1905 reported that the number of Harvey Girls going to the altar had created a severe shortage in waitstaff at Harvey Houses on the Santa Fe Railway line. "These establishments have been drained of their table help," the article proclaimed. "A special sort of girl always has been demanded by the Harvey management, and as the service pays from $25 to $35 a month, with board, room and laundry, along with scores of social privileges, it has been little trouble to keep the supply of help equal to the demand.[22]

"Lately, however, matrimonial fever appears to have swept along the Santa Fe from La Junta to Needles, and as fast as girls are hired they are gobbled up by bearded stockmen, miners, railway men and others, some of whom regard the girls in the light of angels sent to the desert for the express purpose of throwing the influence of womanhood around their lonely lives. As a result, justices of the peace in New Mexico and Arizona have recently struck a mint acting as marriage parsons, and Fred Harvey is anxious to pay bonds for waitresses with proper qualifications."[23]

More than twenty years after Fred Harvey established the first of his dining halls along the Santa Fe Railway line, the corporation was routinely basking in success. In 1915, the restaurants and eating rooms fed some 5,000,000 travelers, and the commissariat furnished over 500,000 pounds of butter; 750,000 pounds of chicken; 4,500,000 pounds of flour; over 5,000,000 pounds of potatoes; and more than 1,500,000 pounds of sugar. It cost the Harvey system $1,000 a day for milk and cream, and the small items like polishes and cleaning materials took $30,000 a year.[24]

In addition to the chain of restaurants from Kansas to California, the Harvey Company had invested in hotels along the same train route. Tourism was on the rise, and executives at the company believed they could offer the same quality overnight accommodations and service travelers had come to expect at the dining halls. Just like the restaurants, the grand hotels would be staffed with Harvey Girls. Patrons flooded the Harvey Company office with complimentary letters about the women who worked at the facilities. "Half the pleasure of the meals at the Harvey Houses are the Harvey Girls," one customer raved. "A Harvey Hotel without a Harvey Girl would be like a home without the wife or mother."[25]

Harvey Hotels did take local boarders, but their first duty was to serve the traveling public. When the gong sounded alerting the hotel employees of the coming train, the Harvey Girls, drilled thoroughly in their duties, took their places to await the tourists. According to the July 2, 1916, edition of the *Atchison Daily Globe*, the hospitality was so genuine and agreeable that travelers "immediately felt refreshed in spirit as well as body." The Harvey Girls moved about as other railway employees for the Santa Fe Railway, from hotel to dining hall, but not so frequently as to be called "migratory."[26]

They were fixtures, becoming units of the communities where fortune located them. In plains and mountain countries, where population was sparse, they were active members of local society. Harvey Girls left such a lasting impression on those who traveled the Santa Fe Railway that some penned poems to express their gratitude. One of those poems appeared in the November 16, 1911, edition of the *Albuquerque Morning Journal*:[27]

> The Santa Fe—that great railway
> From sunset to the break of day,
> Both rare and bright, while trains speed on
> With tireless flight.

Still, as they whirl, with many a swirl
I'm thinking of a Harvey Girl.
She's here and there, just everywhere.
She's ready with a welcome rare.
She's trim and neat and often sweet.
She'll see you get enough to eat.
Her cheerful smile, will quite beguile
Away dull care for many a mile.
Her smiling face will hold its place
All the while the train speeds on apace,
But, ah, how vain when stops the train
At station next she's here again.
She's here and there, just everywhere.
She's ready with a welcome rare.
With silken curls and teeth like pearls—
The dainty, dimpled Harvey Girls.[28]

The Harvey Company managed several Grand Hotels along the Santa Fe Railway route. The El Vaquero in Dodge City, Kansas, was one of the most elegant on the line. The duties of the Harvey Girls employed there were the same as at the other establishments. They were required to maintain the strict code for cleanliness, including cleaning gas-powered lighting fixtures; dusting furniture and woodwork, including baseboards, door frames, and ceiling fans; washing and pressing all linens; providing guests with extra amenities; and keeping rooms neat and comfortable.[29]

The first Harvey House in Dodge City was installed in 1896. The establishment was expanded and remodeled in 1913. The magnificent transformation of the combination depot-hotel structure made it one of the "very best hotels" on the Santa Fe system. The lobby and dining room of the El Vaquero was compared favorably to the finest and highest-priced hotels in the country. The rooms were equipped with private baths, and the atmosphere of luxury was characteristic of the high-grade establishments in metropolitan cities.[30]

Dodge City was the favorite stopping place for hundreds of commercial travelers and railroad ticket buyers. The El Vaquero was the most sought-after hotel in the region. The building was beautiful and included many high-end features, but guests cited the reason for the hostelry's first-class status was the exceptional work done by the Harvey Girls. "They saw to our every request," Mrs. Gerald Fields, a Santa Fe Railway passenger wrote in a letter to the Harvey Company in late 1916. "I'm convinced the Harvey Girls would make even a stay out on the open prairie a delight."[31]

The El Garces in Needles, California, was another Harvey House with a stellar reputation. It was not only a desired destination for railroad passengers but for Harvey Girls as well. The El Garces was named after the early Spanish missionary who came to Needles in 1771. It was often referred to by patrons and employees alike as "Santa Fe's Best." According to the July 4, 1909, edition of the the *Topeka Daily Capital*, "the hotel is a magnificent house, large and elegant, with every convenience." The article called attention to the one-hundred-plus-degree temperatures at the location and noted how comfortable the dry heat was while staying at the El Garces. "No one could mind the heat while admiring the sight of the purple mountains beyond the Colorado River running close to the hotel. The reading room there is unusually large and commodious, is arranged with a swimming pool, gymnasium, and games. Whatever is lacking, the Harvey Girls will try to correct. Here, all is right with the world."[32]

The El Ortiz Harvey Hotel and lunchroom in Lamy, New Mexico, was known as the "littlest hotel in the littlest town" in the Southwest. The village of Lamy was the transfer point for passengers heading to Santa Fe. The Mission Revival–style depot was built by the Atchison, Topeka and Santa Fe Railway in 1909. The Harvey Company constructed El Ortiz in 1910. Among the well-known guests who stayed at El Ortiz were Owen Wister, author of *The Virginian*, and Buffalo Bill Cody.[33]

In January 1911, Cody was passing through the area on his way to Tucson when he decided to spend a few days in New Mexico. According to the January 23, 1911, edition of the *Santa Fe New Mexican*, Cody believed the hotel would make a perfect place for himself and his performers, but only if the Harvey Girls could be a part of the Buffalo Bill Cody Wild West Show cast. Cody was "greatly impressed with the Spanish style of the El Ortiz Hotel," the *Santa Fe New Mexican* article read, "and after he had viewed the placita and seen the various rooms, and toasted his shins in front of the immense fireplace on which reminded him of the frontier day, the great scout and hunter said with a sigh of pleasure, 'Gee, but this would make a cracker jack ranch house.'"[34]

By mid-1910, competitors of the Santa Fe Railway had introduced their own quality train service, but most travelers agreed no other railroad in the world had a system of dining and lodging that could compare with the Harvey Company. No matter what any competing rail line could offer, they would still be minus the Harvey Girls. It was that workforce more than any other factor that promoted passengers to travel the Santa Fe Railway. An article in the July 24, 1911, edition of the *Arizona Republic* further explained ticket buyers' preference.[35]

"A three day trip across a continent is calculated to wear the novelty of travel threadbare, and the relaxation of stopping to have breakfast, luncheon or dinner in an attractive dining room, and stretch one's limbs in a short stroll about a depot, and a well-designed hotel always planned to conform to the prevailing style of architecture, makes a trip which might be otherwise exceedingly tedious a veritable pleasure and a treat to be long remembered. . . ."[36]

"Harvey hotels along the Santa Fe, and the traveler who makes the trip from Chicago to Los Angeles without forming a lasting admiration for the Harvey system, is either a dyspeptic incapable of enjoying the cuisine of the best kitchens in America, or a misanthrope determined to ignore the perfection of a service carried on under the direction of experienced managers who make it their business to please. . . ."[37]

"The waitresses of the Harvey system are not servants. They put plutocrats to shame at times by their unfailing politeness and their refusal to notice the condescending airs of such would-be-aristocratic travelers, as are occasionally transported over the most respectable railroads, caused Hubbard to describe them as 'girls who are never fly, flip, nor fresh, but who give you the attention that never obtrudes, but which is hearty and heartfelt.'"[38]

The Great Depression and motorization of America in the late 1920s resulted in a substantial decline in people traveling by train. Men and women were driving their own automobiles to various destinations across the United States and had the ability to stop and eat and sleep wherever they chose. They weren't relegated to the Harvey establishments along the Santa Fe Railway line. Luxury trains featuring their own dining cars were introduced, and Harvey lunch counters were no longer necessary. By 1939, numerous Harvey Houses were forced to close.[39]

Small towns in the Southwest that were built around the railroad depot and thrived because of the Harvey dining halls and hotels as well as the Harvey Girls who lived and worked around there ceased to be. Like the prairie schooner, the Pony Express rider, and the old cattle trails, the Harvey House system of the Santa Fe was doomed as a part of the passing show. Newspapers across the country lamented their closing.

"The Harvey Houses served a long-felt need in the middle and far west, and their fame was as wide as the Santa Fe," an article in the April 8, 1940, edition of the *Clovis News-Journal* reported. "They were distributed across the country at distances just right for meal time . . . for trains and even motorists.[40]

"For years the Harvey Houses were the rendezvous of those who liked good accommodations on their travels. Few travelers passed them up for even as little as a good cup of coffee. And those good accommodations brought travel to the Santa Fe. Countless miles out on the desert the traveler suddenly ran into a little town, and there, in the midst of drab surroundings was a magnificent hotel where a New York meal might be had for the asking . . . and rather stiff payment.[41]

"But, like many changes that have taken place in other things along the way, the Harvey Houses are being supplanted by the dining car service...a service that is cheaper than operating the big hotels, and more to the liking of travelers.[42]

"So the Santa Fe, or its subsidiary, the Fred Harvey System, is one by one closing the famous Harvey Houses, each of which bore a distinctive name . . . a name that was linked with history of the West. Many have been closed already, and others are slated to go soon, if reports are true.[43]

"I kinda hate to see the Harvey House close, although I've cussed 'em many a time for chargin' ten cents for a cup of coffee and a dime for a cookie to go with it. Food came high to other than railroad employees at the Harvey Houses. The price was almost prohibitive . . . but we patronized them anyway and were proud of them."[44]

The era of traditional Harvey Girls ended at the conclusion of World War II. The service of the Harvey Girls and the influence they had on the American railroad were the subjects of a 1946 motion picture starring Judy Garland and Angela Lansbury. The MGM musical titled *The Harvey Girls* centered around a cheery crew of young women traveling west to open a Harvey House restaurant in order to provide good cooking and wholesome company for railway travelers. The film won an Academy Award for the song "On the Atchison, Topeka and Santa Fe."[45]

The Harvey Car Courier Corps will take you away "into the beckoning, foot-loose distances of New Mexico," reads the Santa Fe Railway brochure on Indian Detours. The brochures were distributed to train travelers crossing the arid Southwest desert in the late 1920s who were looking for adventure and romance.[46]

Indian Detours were created by the Fred Harvey Company in 1925. The popularity of the automobile and the airplane had created a lull in railroad travel. The Harvey Company introduced the detours in hopes of encouraging the public to journey by train to their next vacation destination. The tours were only available for the Southwest part of the country, from the Grand Canyon to Santa Fe. The specialized tours by car were to divert passengers from the train for one to three days and drive them through the "wilderness panoramas" of northern New Mexico to Indian ruin sites and living pueblos.[47]

The drivers of the Harvey vehicles, which included Packards, Franklins, Cadillacs, and White Motor Company buses, were always men. The tour guides or "couriers" were always women. Executives at the Harvey Company believed following the business model of the Harvey Girls would ensure the success of the Indian Detours.[48]

The women selected to be members of the Harvey Car Courier Corps spent weeks training for their positions. In order to be qualified tour guides, they were required to know the archaeological, ethnological, cultural, geological, botanical, historical, and legislative makeup of New Mexico. It was necessary that the information they shared with travelers

The Harvey Company and the Santa Fe Railway teamed after WWI to offer passengers scenic trips off the beaten path. AUTHOR'S COLLECTION

1. Blossom Time in Old Santa Fé.   2. High-piled Taos Pueblo.   3. Patio of State Museum, Santa Fé.
4. Corner of La Fonda Lounge.   5. Glimpse of the Lounge, El Ortis, Lamy
6. Couriercar Drivers.   7. A few Indian-detour courier-hostesses.

{ 47 }   { 48 }   RAND MCNALLY & COMPANY, CHICAGO

The Santa Fe Railway brochure gave patrons a glimpse of what they could experience on an Indian detour. The bottom right image is of a few Indian detour courier-hostesses. AUTHOR'S COLLECTION

was accurate. The couriers attended lectures and participated in trips along the detour trail. According to the March 12, 1975, edition of the *Santa Fe New Mexican*, most of the Harvey Car Courier Corps members found the work interesting. Aside from teaching school, there were very few interesting jobs for women post–World War I. Couriers earned $150 a month, $160 a month if they spoke a foreign language and could communicate with travelers from other countries.[49]

Among the well-known individuals who took advantage of the Indian Detours were Albert Einstein, John D. Rockefeller, Will Rogers, and Guglielmo Marconi, the inventor of the wireless telegraph.[50]

The Harvey Couriers were required to dress in Navaho-style costumes while giving the tours. The authentic outfit consisted of velveteen skirt, concha belts, and squash blossom necklaces.[51]

The tours originated from the Harvey Houses: the Castaneda in Las Vegas, New Mexico; the Alvarado in Albuquerque; the Ortiz in Lamy; and the Navajo in Gallup. The most popular detour trips were to the Painted Desert, the Petrified Forest, and the Indian pueblos in Taos and Santa Clara. The cost for the tours ranged from ten dollars to fourteen dollars a day.[52]

The Great Depression brought about the end of the Indian Detours and the Harvey Couriers.

CHAPTER 15

The Business and Professional
Women's Club

In July 1927, Pearl Matlock, assistant manager of the Fred Harvey Company advertising department, helped organize train travel for more than one thousand delegates of the Business and Professional Women's Club. The career women were making their way from New York to Oakland, California, for the national convention. The train made stops along the way to collect representatives of the organization, and at each stop reporters were waiting to cover the momentous trip. Pearl was one of the Harvey Company's employees as well as the national chairwoman of the Business and Professional Women's Club.[1]

By the summer of 1927, the organization had more than forty-five thousand members. Its goal was to call attention to the "broadening effect of women's contact in businesses and promote higher efficiency among them."[2] An article about the event in the February 20, 1927, edition of the *Albuquerque Journal* explained that "[b]usinesswomen in the East, who did not fully realize and appreciate the historic and artistic Southwest, would have an opportunity on the train trip to acquaint themselves with the progress made in that part of the country."[3]

Key delegates of the Business and Professional Women's Club acted as "conductors" when the train traveled through their respective home states. The BPW transcontinental train was scheduled for extended stopovers in Colorado, Santa Fe, and at the Grand Canyon.

The July 14, 1927, edition of the *Arizona Daily Star* covered the group's arrival into Flagstaff on July 13. "When the train jolted to a stop

Pearl Matlock, assistant manager of the Fred Harvey Company
advertising department AUTHOR'S COLLECTION

at 3 A.M., twenty BPW/AZ 'cowboys' dressed in ten-gallon hats, neck-erchiefs, white blouses, blue bobby skirts, guns, and holsters pretended to hold up the train," the article explained. "Once on board, they distributed copper and wooden souvenirs, *Progressive Arizona* magazine, a half a train car load of cantaloupes, and other Arizona fruit to passengers."[4]

When the train arrived at the Grand Canyon at 6:00 a.m., Governor George W. Hunt and other staff officials welcomed the organization's president to Arizona. Hopi Indians performed ceremonial dances, and cowboys staged a small rodeo. After disembarking from the train, passengers walked or drove around the canyon rim while others rode mules a short distance down the Bright Angel Trail. The day ended when the Santa Fe Railway transported the women to a banquet at the Harvey House hotel, the El Tovar.[5]

The first all-women railroad party to cross the Continental Divide arrived in Oakland on July 21, 1927. The organization's motto "Better Business Women for a Better Business World," typified all the club represented. It would eventually become the largest women's organization in the world.[6]

Notes

Introduction
1 *Godey's Lady's Book and Magazine*, August 1869
2 *San Francisco Examiner*, May 7, 1869; *Baltimore Sun*, May 17, 1869
3 *Godey's Lady's Book and Magazine*, August 1869
4 https://www.nrrhof.org/single-post/2018/03/08/Looking-Back-Women-in
-Railroading
5 Ibid.
6 Ibid.
7 Ibid.
8 Ibid.
9 *Leavenworth Times*, June 22, 1905
10 *San Francisco Call Chronicle Examiner*, May 4, 1906
11 *Purple Passage: The Life of Mrs. Frank Leslie*, pp. 80–91
12 Ibid.
13 *The Ladies' Book of Etiquette and Manual of Politeness*, pp. 72–76
14 *Riverside Daily Press*, July 10, 1886
15 Ibid.
16 Ibid.

Chapter 1: The Telegraphers
1 *Philadelphia Inquirer*, December 28, 1909; *Statesman Journal*, May 15, 1900
2 Ibid., *Philadelphia Inquirer*, December 28, 1909
3 *Times*, May 7, 1900
4 *Pittsburgh Evening Chronicle*, August 8, 1861; *Harper's Magazine*, August 1, 1873
5 *How Women Can Make Money*, pp. 100–101
6 www.nationalrailroadhalloffame.org
7 *Spirit of the Age*, July 26, 1876; *Rutland Daily Herald*, July 15, 1876
8 Ibid.; *Telegrapher*, July 15, 1876
9 *Telegrapher*, September 23, 1876
10 www.ancestry.com; *Santa Maria Times*, March 8, 1877
11 *Press Tribune*, April 30, 1999
12 Ibid.; *Press Tribune*, October 27, 1995

13 Ibid.
14 Ibid.
15 *Los Angeles Times*, May 5, 1958
16 Ibid.
17 Ibid.
18 Ibid.
19 Ibid.
20 *Deming Headlight*, October 14, 2004
21 *Southern Illinoisan*, October 18, 1971
22 *Los Angeles Times*, August 20, 1924
23 *San Francisco Examiner*, July 31, 1955
24 Ibid.
25 http://digital.library.pitt.edu/u/ulmanuscripts/pdf/3175061545012.pdf
26 *San Francisco Examiner*, July 31, 1955
27 *Buffalo Sunday Morning News*, January 11, 1903
28 *Railroad Magazine*, April 1950
29 Ibid.
30 *Ma Kiley: The Life of a Railroad Telegrapher*, pp. 53–55
31 Ibid.; *Railroad Magazine*, April 1950
32 Ibid.; *Ma Kiley: The Life of a Railroad Telegrapher*, pp. 53–55
33 *Railroad Magazine*, April 1950; *The Order of Railroad Telegraphers: A Study in Trade Unionism and Collective Bargaining*, pp. 88–90
34 *Ma Kiley: The Life of a Railroad Telegrapher*, pp. 59–61
35 Ibid., pp. 61–64
36 Ibid., pp. 66–68
37 Ibid., pp. 68–70
38 Ibid., pp. 76–79
39 Ibid.
40 Ibid.
41 Ibid.
42 Ibid., pp. 82–84
43 Ibid., pp. 91–93; *El Paso Times*, September 24, 2000
44 *Nevada State Journal*, March 4, 1933
45 Ibid., *Nevada State Journal*, October 29, 1952

Chapter 2: Sarah Kidder: The Railroad President

1 *San Francisco Call*, April 11, 1901
2 *History of Nevada County, California*, pp. 129–130, 222; *Gold Cities: Grass Valley and Nevada City*, pp. 39–40
3 *Nevada County Narrow Gauge Railroad*, pp. 81–83

4 *Oakdale Leader*, September 20, 1901
5 Ibid.
6 *Nevada County Narrow Gauge Railroad*, pp. 50–53
7 Ibid.
8 Ibid., pp. 48–51
9 Ibid., pp. 81–83
10 Ibid., pp. 71–78
11 Ibid.
12 Ibid., pp. 71–78, *San Francisco Call*, June 14, 1901
13 *Nevada County Narrow Gauge Railroad*, pp. 71–78
14 Ibid., 82–97
15 Ibid.
16 *San Francisco Call*, April 10, 1913
17 *Republic*, February 27, 1912
18 *Nevada County Narrow Gauge Railroad*, pp. 81–82
19 Ibid.
20 *Nevada County Narrow Gauge Railroad*, pp. 82–97
21 *San Francisco Chronicle*, November 10, 1908
22 *San Francisco Bulletin*, July 8, 1908
23 *Nevada County Narrow Gauge Railroad*, pp. 82–97
24 *Evening Herald*, November 2, 1911
25 *San Francisco Call*, May 11, 1913; *Nevada County Narrow Gauge Railroad*, pp. 82–97
26 Ibid., *Province*, April 3, 1906
27 *San Francisco Examiner*, December 14, 1913
28 Ibid.
29 *San Francisco Chronicle*, March 8, 1914; March 27, 1914
30 *San Francisco Examiner*, September 30, 1933
31 *Neosho Daily News*, June 30, 1942

Chapter 3: Helen Hunt Jackson: The Poet's Railroad Tour

1 https://www.econedlink.org/wp-content/uploads/legacy/719_railroads1.pdf
2 *Helen Hunt Jackson: A Literary Life*, pp. 25, 109–111
3 Ibid., pp. 11–12; *Colorado Springs Gazette-Telegraph*, March 23, 1972
4 *Helen Hunt Jackson: A Literary Life*, pp. 75–77
5 Ibid., pp. 139–141
6 Ibid., pp. 109–111; *Colorado Springs Gazette-Telegraph*, March 23, 1972
7 *Bits of Travel at Home*, pp. 3–16
8 Ibid.
9 Ibid.

10 Ibid.
11 Ibid.
12 Ibid.
13 Ibid.
14 Ibid.
15 Ibid.
16 Ibid.
17 Ibid.
18 Ibid., pp. 17–27
19 Ibid.
20 Ibid.
21 Ibid., pp. 17–27
22 Ibid., pp. 28–35
23 Ibid.
24 Ibid.
25 Ibid.
26 Ibid.
27 Ibid.
28 Ibid., 36–68
29 Ibid.
30 Ibid.
31 Ibid.
32 Ibid.
33 Ibid.
34 Ibid.
35 Ibid.
36 Ibid.
37 Ibid.
38 *Scribner's Monthly Magazine*, May 1873
39 *Morning Journal-Courier*, August 13, 1885; *Colorado Springs Gazette-Telegraph*, March 23, 1972
40 *Colorado Springs Gazette-Telegraph*, March 23, 1972; *Bits of Travel at Home*, pp. 209–211
41 Ibid.; *Colorado Springs Gazette-Telegraph*, March 23, 1972

Chapter 4: Laura Bullion: The Wild Bunch Train Robber

1 *Anaconda Standard*, July 10, 1901; *Spokane Chronicle*, July 8, 1901; *Tacoma Times*, September 2, 1913; *Wild Bunch Women*, pp. 77–80
2 *Tacoma Times*, September 2, 1913; *Anaconda Standard*, July 10, 1901
3 *Anaconda Standard*, July 10, 1901; *Tacoma Times*, September 2, 1913

4 *Tacoma Times*, September 2, 1913
5 *Great Falls Tribune*, July 4, 1901
6 Ibid.; *Capital Journal*, November 30, 1901
7 *Capital Journal*, November 30, 1901
8 *Great Falls Tribune*, July 4, 1901
9 Ibid.; *Capital Journal*, November 30, 1901
10 *Ironton County Register*, July 11, 1901
11 *Saint Paul Globe*, July 27, 1901
12 Ibid.
13 Ibid.
14 Ibid.
15 Ibid.
16 Ibid.
17 *Wichita Beacon*, December 10, 1897; *Alexandria Gazette*, December 10, 1897; *Wild Bunch Women*, pp. 77–80
18 *Encyclopedia Western Lawmen and Outlaws*, pp. 58–59; *Wild Bunch Women*, pp. 77–80
19 Ibid.; *Encyclopedia Western Lawmen and Outlaws*, pp. 58–59
20 *Hell's Half Acre*, pp. 248–249
21 *Encyclopedia Western Lawmen and Outlaws*, pp. 58–59; *Wild Bunch Women*, pp. 77–80
22 *Great Falls Tribune*, November 7, 1918
23 *Statesman Journal*, November 30, 1901; *Minneapolis Journal*, November 8, 1901
24 *St. Louis Republic*, November 8, 1901
25 *San Angelo Press*, November 15, 1901
26 Ibid.
27 Ibid.
28 *Evening Times Republican*, November 18, 1901; *Los Angeles Times*, November 8, 1901
29 Ibid.
30 *Saint Paul Globe*, November 16, 1901
31 Ibid.
32 *Anaconda Standard*, December 12, 1901
33 Ibid.
34 Ibid.
35 *Inter Ocean*, December 8, 1901
36 *Ogden Standard*, December 12, 1901; *Butte Daily Post*, December 13, 1901
37 *St. Louis Post-Dispatch*, June 12, 1904
38 Ibid.; *Seguin Gazette Enterprise*, December 14, 1914
39 *St. Louis Post-Dispatch*, September 21, 1905

40 Ibid.
41 Ibid.
42 Ibid.
43 Ibid.
44 Ibid.
45 Ibid.
46 Ibid.
47 Ibid.
48 *St. Louis Star & Times*, January 17, 1911; *Inter Ocean*, March 6, 1912
49 Ibid.
50 *El Paso Herald*, March 14, 1912
51 Ibid.
52 Ibid.
53 Ibid.
54 *Detroit Free Press*, March 15, 1912
55 *Seguin Gazette Enterprise*, December 14, 1994
56 *El Paso Herald-Post*, October 21, 1961; *Wild Bunch Women*, pp. 77–80

Chapter 5: Lillie Langtry: The Jersey Lily and the LaLee
1 *The American Railroad Passenger Car*, pp. 226–227; *The Days I Knew*, pp. 177–178; *The Man Who Robbed the Robber Barons*, pp. 118–128
2 *The Days I Knew*, pp. 15–18
3 *Los Angeles Herald*, May 6, 1888
4 *The Days I Knew*, pp. 177–180
5 Ibid.
6 Ibid.
7 Ibid.
8 Ibid.
9 Ibid.
10 *Los Angeles Herald*, May 6, 1888
11 *Chicago Tribune*, February 21, 1888
12 Ibid.
13 Ibid.
14 *St. Joseph Gazette-Herald*, April 12, 1888
15 *The Days I Knew*, pp. 182–184
16 Ibid.
17 Ibid.
18 Ibid.
19 *Utah Daily Union*, June 12, 1888
20 Ibid.

21 Ibid.
22 *The Days I Knew*, pp. 8–12, 189, 285
23 Ibid.; *Denton Record Chronicle*, August 27, 1937
24 Ibid.; *The Days I Knew*, pp. 8–12, 189, 285
25 Ibid.; *Denton Record Chronicle*, August 27, 1937
26 Ibid.; *The Days I Knew*, pp. 8–12, 189, 285
27 Ibid.; *Denton Record Chronicle*, August 27, 1937
28 Ibid.; *The Days I Knew*, pp. 8–12, 189, 285
29 Ibid.; *Denton Record Chronicle*, August 27, 1937
30 Ibid.; *The Days I Knew*, pp. 8–12, 189, 285
31 *The Days I Knew*, pp. 192–197
32 Ibid.
33 Ibid.
34 Ibid.
35 Ibid.
36 Ibid.

Chapter 6: Mary Pennington: The Creator of the Modern Refrigerator Boxcar

1 *Leavenworth Times*, October 19, 1917
2 http://www.hevac-heritage.org/built_environment/biographies/surnames_M-R/pennington/P1-PENNINGTON.pdf
3 Ibid.
4 *Pittsburgh Post*, December 30, 2002; *Green Bay Press-Gazette*, November 28, 1902
5 *Chicago Tribune*, April 2, 1905; *Standard Union*, October 27, 1905; *Oshkosh Northwestern*, October 20, 1906
6 http://www.hevac-heritage.org/built_environment/biographies/surnames_M-R/pennington/P1-PENNINGTON.pdf
7 *Washington Post*, December 4, 1908
8 Ibid.
9 http://prototyperails.com/PDF/Abstracts_rev04_2019.pdf; *Dayton Daily News*, July 20, 1928; *The American Railroad Freight Car*, pp. 242–243
10 *The American Railroad Freight Car*, pp. 242–243
11 *Oregon Daily Journal*, March 20, 1910
12 Ibid.
13 Ibid.
14 Ibid.
15 Ibid.
16 Ibid.
17 Ibid.

18 *Atlanta Constitution*, August 17, 1930
19 *Refrigeration Nation: A History of Ice, Appliances, and Enterprise in America (Studies in Industry and Society)*, pp. 114–117
20 *Salina Daily Union*, January 19, 1922; *St. Louis Post-Dispatch*, December 29, 1952
21 *Times Tribune*, June 23, 1921
22 *St. Louis Post-Dispatch*, December 29, 1952
23 *Tampa Tribune*, December 30, 1952

Chapter 7: Miriam Leslie: The Journalist Riding the Rails
1 *California: A Pleasure Trip from Gotham to the Golden Gate*, pp. 15–18; *Frank Leslie's Illustrated Newspaper*, July 7, 1877; *Out West on the Overland Train*, pp. 12–13
2 Ibid.
3 Ibid.
4 *California: A Pleasure Trip from Gotham to the Golden Gate*, pp. 15–18; *Frank Leslie's Illustrated Newspaper*, July 7, 1877; *Smithsonian Magazine*, December 11, 2013
5 *California: A Pleasure Trip from Gotham to the Golden Gate*, pp. 15–18; *Frank Leslie's Illustrated Newspaper*, July 7, 1877; *Out West on the Overland Train*, pp. 12–13
6 *San Francisco Examiner*, April 18, 1877
7 *Purple Passage: The Life of Mrs. Frank Leslie*, pp. 5–7
8 Ibid., pp. 7–13
9 Ibid., pp. 19–23; *Lola Montez: A Life*, pp. 344–348
10 *Purple Passage: The Life of Mrs. Frank Leslie*, pp. 26–31
11 Ibid., 39–41
12 Ibid., 68–71
13 Ibid., 78–89; *California: A Pleasure Trip from Gotham to the Golden Gate*, pp. 19–20; *Out West on the Overland Train*, pp. 12–13
14 *Purple Passage: The Life of Mrs. Frank Leslie*, pp. 78–89; *California: A Pleasure Trip from Gotham to the Golden Gate*, pp. 19–20; *Out West on the Overland Train*, pp. 12–13
15 *California: A Pleasure Trip from Gotham to the Golden Gate*, pp. 28–32; *Out West on the Overland Train*, pp. 14–17
16 Ibid.
17 Ibid.
18 Ibid.
19 *Weekly Davenport Democrat*, April 26, 1877
20 *Chicago Tribune*, April 13, 1877

21 *California: A Pleasure Trip from Gotham to the Golden Gate*, pp. 27–34; *Out West on the Overland Train*, pp. 20–22

22 *California: A Pleasure Trip from Gotham to the Golden Gate*, pp. 27–34

23 Ibid.; *Out West on the Overland Train*, pp. 22–25

24 Ibid.; *Out West on the Overland Train*, pp. 28–31

25 *California: A Pleasure Trip from Gotham to the Golden Gate*, pp. 43–51; *Out West on the Overland Train*, pp. 37–41

26 *California: A Pleasure Trip from Gotham to the Golden Gate*, pp. 43–54; *Out West on the Overland Train*, pp. 64–67

27 *California: A Pleasure Trip from Gotham to the Golden Gate*, pp. 54–56; *Out West on the Overland Train*, pp. 72–74

28 Ibid.

29 Ibid.

30 *California: A Pleasure Trip from Gotham to the Golden Gate*, pp. 63–65; *Out West on the Overland Train*, pp. 78–80

31 Ibid.

32 *California: A Pleasure Trip from Gotham to the Golden Gate*, pp. 69–72; *Out West on the Overland Train*, pp. 90–92

33 Ibid.

34 Ibid.

35 *Desert News*, May 2, 1877

36 *California: A Pleasure Trip from Gotham to the Golden Gate*, pp. 85–90; *Out West on the Overland Train*, pp. 113–118

37 Ibid.

38 Ibid.

39 Ibid.

40 *California: A Pleasure Trip from Gotham to the Golden Gate*, pp. 96–101; *Out West on the Overland Train*, pp. 134–137

41 Ibid.

42 Ibid.

43 *Reno Gazette-Journal*, May 29, 1877; *California: A Pleasure Trip from Gotham to the Golden Gate*, pp. 96–101; *Out West on the Overland Train*, pp. 134–137

44 *California: A Pleasure Trip from Gotham to the Golden Gate*, pp. 112–115; *Out West on the Overland Train*, pp. 138–144

45 Ibid.

46 Ibid.

47 *California: A Pleasure Trip from Gotham to the Golden Gate*, pp. 121–125; *Out West on the Overland Train*, pp. 166–169

48 Ibid.

49 Ibid.

50 Ibid.
51 *California: A Pleasure Trip from Gotham to the Golden Gate*, pp. 132–140; *Out West on the Overland Train*, pp. 172–178
52 Ibid.
53 Ibid.
54 Ibid.
55 *California: A Pleasure Trip from Gotham to the Golden Gate*, pp. 234–238
56 Ibid.
57 *Times*, December 18, 1877
58 *California: A Pleasure Trip from Gotham to the Golden Gate*, pp. 132–139
59 Ibid.
60 Ibid.
61 Ibid.
62 *Springville Journal*, September 28, 1878
63 *Purple Passage: The Life of Mrs. Frank Leslie*, pp. 232–233
64 Ibid.

Chapter 8: Women vs. the Railroad: The Fight for Fairness on the Rails
1 *Daily Republican*, October 24, 1929
2 Ibid.
3 *150 Years of North American Railroads*, pp. 8–13
4 *American Railroad Passenger Car*, pp. 15, 203
5 *Parsons Daily Eclipse*, February 23, 1893; *Law & History Review*, pp. 261–316
6 Ibid.
7 Ibid.; *Evening Messenger*, February 27, 1893
8 *Courier Journal*, November 29, 1881
9 *Chicago-Kent Law Review*, pp. 993–999
10 *Courier Journal*, November 29, 1881
11 Ibid.
12 *Reading Times*, April 20, 1882; *LeRoy Reporter*, April 29, 1882
13 *Louisville Bulletin*, September 13, 1881
14 *San Antonio Light*, October 20, 1882
15 *Cincinnati Enquirer*, August 25, 1882

Chapter 9: Olive Dennis: The Railroad Civil Engineer
1 *Passage to Union: How the Railroads Transformed American Life, 1829-1929*, pp. 27–30
2 *Pittsburgh Sun Telegraph*, April 27, 1940
3 Ibid.

4 *Evening Sun*, February 24, 1921
5 Ibid.
6 Ibid.
7 Ibid.
8 Ibid.
9 *Leader-Telegram*, May 22, 1947
10 Ibid.
11 https://www.engineergirl.org/125278/Olive-Dennis
12 Ibid.
13 *Baltimore Sun*, November 7, 1957
14 *Newark Advocate*, January 10, 1947
15 Ibid.
16 *Star Democrat*, January 17, 1947; https://www.engineergirl.org/125278/Olive-Dennis
17 *Star Democrat*, January 17, 1947; https://www.engineergirl.org/125278/Olive-Dennis
18 *Star Democrat*, January 17, 1947; https://www.engineergirl.org/125278/Olive-Dennis
19 *Cumberland Evening Times*, November 7, 1957
20 Ibid.

Chapter 10: Phoebe Snow: The Railroad Pinup Girl

1 *The Delaware, Lackawanna & Western Railroad, the Route of Phoebe Snow, in the Twentieth Century, 1899-1960: Part One*, pp. 17–28; *Star Press*, October 6, 1963
2 Ibid.
3 *Winnipeg Tribune*, January 4, 1947; *The Delaware, Lackawanna & Western Railroad, the Route of Phoebe Snow, in the Twentieth Century, 1899-1960: Part One*, pp. 17–28
4 *Tallahassee Democrat*, January 28, 1963
5 *Star Press*, October 6, 1963
6 *New York Herald*, July 9, 1922
7 *The Delaware, Lackawanna & Western Railroad, the Route of Phoebe Snow, in the Twentieth Century, 1899-1960: Part One*, pp. 17–28; *Star Press*, October 6, 1963

Chapter 11: Julia Bulette: The Madam Honored by the Railroad

1 *Wicked Women: Notorious, Mischievous, and Wayward Ladies from the Old West*, pp. 33–39; *Bakersfield Californian*, October 25, 1892
2 *Janesville Gazette*, June 9, 1868

3 Ibid., *Wicked Women: Notorious, Mischievous, and Wayward Ladies from the Old West*, pp. 33–39

4 *The Red Light Ladies of Virginia City*, pp. 49–53; *Janesville Gazette*, June 9, 1868

5 *Reno Gazette-Journal*, November 9, 1955

6 Ibid.

7 Ibid.

8 Ibid.; *Janesville Gazette*, June 9, 1868

9 *Janesville Gazette*, June 9, 1868

10 *Bristol Daily Courier*, October 17, 1959; https://alchetron.com/Julia-Bulette

Chapter 12: Mary Colter: The Harvey House Architect

1 *Arizona Daily Star*, May 20, 1930

2 *Arizona Republican*, May 15, 1930; *Preservation Magazine*, July/August 1997; *Mary Colter: Architect of the Southwest*, pp. 164–185

3 Ibid.; *Arizona Republican*, May 15, 1930; *Preservation Magazine*, July/August 1997

4 *Railroad Heritage*, Spring 2015; *Mary Colter: Architect of the Southwest*, pp. 9–17

5 Drawings were donated to the Little Bighorn Battlefield National Monument in Montana.

6 Ibid.; www.ancestry.com

7 *Mary Colter: Architect of the Southwest*, pp. 34–55

8 Ibid.

9 *The Harvey Girls*, pp. 28–39

10 *Albuquerque Citizen*, May 10, 1902

11 *Mary Colter: Architect of the Southwest*, pp. 53–57

12 Ibid.; *Railroad Heritage*, Spring 2015

13 *Mary Colter: Architect of the Southwest*, pp. 64–68

14 *Arizona Daily Sun*, April 6, 1955

15 Ibid.; *Greeley Daily Tribune*, November 6, 1975

16 Ibid.; *Arizona Daily Sun*, April 6, 1955

17 *The Harvey Girls*, pp. 120–122; *Mary Colter: Architect of the Southwest*, pp. 77–78; *Albuquerque Journal*, August 19, 1911

18 *Albuquerque Journal*, August 19, 1911; *Mary Colter: Architect of the Southwest*, pp. 77–78

19 *Arizona Republic*, July 24, 1911

20 Ibid.

21 Ibid.

22 Ibid.

23 Ibid.
24 *Santa Fe New Mexican,* January 23, 1911
25 *Star Gazette,* October 19, 1914
26 *Atchison Daily Globe,* November 6, 1914
27 *Mary Colter: Architect of the Southwest,* pp. 90–96
28 *Mary Colter: Architect of the Southwest,* pp. 90–96; *Asbury Park Press,* February 10, 2002
29 *Mary Colter: Architect of the Southwest,* pp. 90–96
30 *Ogden Standard,* May 29, 1915
31 *Mary Colter: Architect of the Southwest,* pp. 90–96; *Statesman Journal,* December 23, 2001; *Los Angeles Times,* November 7, 1919
32 *Mary Colter: Architect of the Southwest,* pp. 90–96; *Los Angeles Time,* November 7, 1919
33 *Grand Canyon Outings,* June 1938
34 *Mary Colter: Architect of the Southwest,* pp. 108–113
35 Ibid.
36 *Grand Canyon Outings,* June 1938; *Topeka State Journal,* July 15, 1922
37 *Mary Colter: Architect of the Southwest,* pp. 122–124
38 *Evening Herald,* January 1, 1922
39 *Mary Colter: Architect of the Southwest,* pp. 128–144
40 Ibid.
41 *El Paso Times,* May 29, 1923
42 Ibid.
43 *Mary Colter: Architect of the Southwest,* pp. 193–199; *Grand Canyon Outings,* June 1938
44 Ibid.; *Mary Colter: Architect of the Southwest,* pp. 193–199
45 Ibid.; *Grand Canyon Outings,* June 1938
46 *San Bernardino County Sun,* May 22, 1933; *Dayton Daily News,* May 19, 1933
47 Ibid.; *San Bernardino County Sun,* May 22, 1933; *Chillicothe Constitution-Tribune,* May 18, 1933
48 *Railroad Heritage,* Spring 2015; *Preservation Magazine,* July/August 1997

Chapter 13: Mary Louise Lawser: The Santa Fe Railroad Muralist
1 http://moorewomenartists.org/philad; www.ancestry.com; *Philadelphia Inquirer,* March 29, 1945; Historical File, California State Railroad Museum
2 http://moorewomenartists.org/philad
3 *Morning Call,* May 5, 1939; Historical File, California State Railroad Museum
4 *Morning Call,* May 27, 1938; Historical File, California State Railroad Museum

5 Ibid.; *The Art of the Streamliner*, pp. 153–156
6 *San Francisco Examiner*, March 19, 1949
7 Historical File, California State Railroad Museum; *Palm Beach Post*, March 2, 1947; http://calzephyr.railfan.net

Chapter 14: The Harvey Girls: The Railroads' Hospitality Ambassadors
1 *Kansas City Journal-Post*, February 29, 1897; *Daily Advertiser*, July 3, 1952; *Daily Item*, December 24, 2017
2 *Ravalli Republic*, May 10, 1899
3 Ibid.
4 Ibid.
5 Ibid.
6 *The Harvey Girls*, pp. 33–36; *Cuba Review*, November 20, 1903
7 *Salt Lake Tribune*, February 10, 1910
8 *Albuquerque Journal*, June 21, 1910; *Deming Headlight*, December 17, 1909
9 *The Harvey Girls*, pp. 35–38; https://www.kshs.org/kansapedia/fred-harvey/15507
10 *Topeka Daily Capital*, March 22, 1890
11 *Leavenworth Times*, February 12, 1901; *The Harvey Girls*, pp. 38–42
12 *San Bernardino County Sun*, April 27, 1990; *Des Moines Tribune*, November 20, 1968; *The Harvey Girls*, pp. 55–58
13 *The Harvey Girls*, pp. 90–91; *Appetite for America: Fred Harvey and the Business of Civilizing the Wild West—One Meal at a Time*, pp. 91–94
14 *Gazette*, February 19, 1952; *The Harvey Girls*, pp. 56–60
15 *Our Fifty States*, pp. 137–140
16 *Gazette*, February 19, 1952
17 *The Harvey Girls*, pp. 64–65
18 Ibid., pp. 85–87
19 *Times*, May 30, 1937; *Times*, April 24, 1939
20 *The Harvey Girls*, pp. 93–94; *Pittsburgh Sun-Telegraph*, May 29, 1941
21 *American Weekly*, August 15, 1948
22 *Bakersfield Daily Report*, August 2, 1905
23 Ibid.
24 *Charlotte Observer*, March 30, 1916
25 *Atchison Daily Globe*, July 2, 1916
26 Ibid.
27 *Albuquerque Journal*, November 16, 1911
28 Ibid.
29 *Dodge City Kansas Journal*, March 27, 1913; *Dodge City Kansas Journal*, January 1, 1915

30 Ibid.
31 *The Harvey Girls*, pp. 35–38; https://www.kshs.org/kansapedia/fred-harvey/15507
32 *Topeka Daily Capital*, July 4, 1909
33 *Albuquerque Journal*, August 19, 1911
34 *Santa Fe New Mexican*, January 23, 1911
35 *Arizona Republic*, July 24, 1911
36 Ibid.
37 Ibid.
38 Ibid.
39 *Emporium Gazette*, February 1, 1937
40 *Clovis-News Journal*, April 8, 1940
41 Ibid.
42 Ibid.
43 Ibid.
44 Ibid.
45 *Indianapolis Star*, January 27, 1946
46 *Carlsbad Current-Argus*, February 10, 1928
47 Ibid.; https://santafeselection.com/blog/2014/06/21/Indian-detours-now
48 *Santa Fe New Mexican*, March 12, 1978
49 Ibid.
50 Ibid.
51 https://santafeselection.com/blog/2014/06/21/Indian-detours-now
52 *Albuquerque Journal*, February 6, 1928

Chapter 15: The Business and Professional Women's Club

1 *Muncie Evening Press*, September 11, 1926
2 *Smoke Signal*, March 2018
3 *Albuquerque Journal*, February 20, 1927
4 *Arizona Daily Star*, July 14, 1927
5 *Smoke Signal*, March 2018; *Arizona Republic*, June 20, 1927
6 *Arizona Republic*, July 14, 1927

Bibliography

BOOKS

Beebee, Lucius. *Highball: A Pageant of Trains.* New York: D. Appleton-Century Co., 1943.

Berke, Arnold. *Mary Colter: Architect of the Southwest.* New York: Princeton Architectural Press, 2002.

Best, Gerald M. *Nevada County Narrow Gauge.* Berkeley, CA: Howell-North Books, 1965.

Burman, Shirley. *She's Been Working on the Railroad.* New York: Lodestar Books, 1997.

Churella, Albert J. *The Pennsylvania Railroad, Volume 1: Building an Empire, 1846–1917 (American Business, Politics, and Society).* Philadelphia: University of Pennsylvania Press, 2012.

Enss, Chris. *Wicked Women: Notorious, Mischievous, and Wayward Ladies from the Old West.* Guilford, CT: TwoDot, 2015.

Fitzsimons, Bernard. *150 Years of North American Railroads.* Secaucus, NJ: Chartwell Books, 1982.

Fried, Stephen. *Appetite for America: Fred Harvey and the Business of Civilizing the Wild West—One Meal at a Time.* New York: Bantam, 2011.

Gordon, Sarah H. *Passage to Union: How the Railroads Transformed American Life, 1829–1929.* Chicago: Ivan R. Dee, 1998.

Hartley, Florence. *The Ladies' Book of Etiquette and Manual of Politeness.* London, England: Hesperus Press, 2015.

Hornung, Clarence P. *Wheels across America.* New York: A. S. Barnes and Company, 1959.

Jackson, Helen Hunt. *Bits of Travel at Home: California, New England, Colorado.* Boston: Robert Brothers Publishing, 1878.

Jepson, Thomas C. *Ma Kiley: The Life of a Railroad Telegrapher.* El Paso, Texas: Texas Western Press, 1997.

Johnston, Bob, and Joe Welsh. *The Art of the Streamliner.* New York: Metro Books, 2001.

Langtry, Lillie. *The Days I Knew.* New York: George H. Doran Company, 1925.

Leslie, Frank Mrs. *California: A Pleasure Trip from Gotham to the Golden Gate, April, May, June 1877.* New York: G. W. Carleton & Co. Publishers, 1877.

Logan, Andy. *The Man Who Robbed the Robber Barons: The Story of Colonel William d'Alton Mann: War Hero, Profiteer, Inventor and Blackmailer Extraordinary*. New York: W. W. Norton, 1965.

Morley, Jim, and Doris Foley. *Gold Cities: Grass Valley and Nevada City*. Berkeley, CA: Howell-North Books, 1965.

Nash, Jay R. *Encyclopedia of Western Lawmen and Outlaws*. New York: First Paragon House, 1989.

Penny, Virginia. *How Women Can Make Money*. New York: Arno Press, 1870.

Phillips, Kate. *Helen Hunt Jackson: A Literary Life*. Berkeley: University of California Press, 2003.

Poling-Kempes, Lesley. *The Harvey Girls: Women Who Opened the West*. Cambridge, MA: Da Capo Press, 1989.

Rayburn, Richard, and Janet Hale. *Our Fifty States*. Garden Grove, CA: Teacher Created Resources, 1994.

Rees, Jonathan. *Refrigeration Nation: A History of Ice, Appliances, and Enterprise in America (Studies in Industry and Society)*. Baltimore: John Hopkins University Press, 2016.

Reinhardt, Richard. *Out West on the Overland Train: Across the Continent Excursion with Leslie's Magazine in 1877 and the Overland Trip in 1967*. Palo Alto, CA: The American West Publishing Company, 1967.

Rutter, Michael. *Wild Bunch Women*. Guilford, CT: TwoDot, 2003.

Selcer, Richard F. *Hell's Half Acre*. Fort Worth: Texas Christian University Press, 1991.

Seymour, Bruce. *Lola Montez: A Life*. New Haven, CT: Yale University Press, 1996.

Stern, Madeleine P. *Purple Passage: The Life of Mrs. Frank Leslie*. Norman: University of Oklahoma Press, 1953.

Thomas, Taber T. *The Delaware, Lackawanna & Western Railroad, the Route of Phoebe Snow, in the Twentieth Century, 1899–1960: Part One*. Muncy, PA: T. T. Taber III, 1980.

Thompson, Thomas, and Albert West. *History of Nevada County California*. Berkeley, CA: Howell-North Books, 1880.

White, John H. *The American Railroad Passenger Car, Part 2*. Baltimore: John Hopkins University Press, 1978.

White, John H. *The American Railroad Freight Car: From the Wood-Car Era to the Coming of Steel*. Baltimore: John Hopkins University Press, 1983.

Williams III, George. *The Red Light Ladies of Virginia City, Nevada*. Carson City, NV: Tree by the River Publishing, 1984.

MAGAZINES, JOURNALS, AND OTHER SOURCES

Coolidge, Susan. "A Few Hints on the California Journey." *Scribner's Monthly Magazine* (May 1873).

Grand Canyon Outings, Santa Fe Train Adventures Pamphlet, June 1938.

Historical File, California State Railroad Museum.

Jepson, Thomas C. "A Look into the Future: Women Railroad Telegraphers and Station Agents in Pennsylvania 1855–1960." *Pennsylvania History: A Journal of Mid-Atlantic Studies* 76, no. 2 (2009).

Kelly, John. "Mary Colter: Her Life." *Railroad Heritage* (Spring 2015).

Kiley, Ma. "The Bug & I." *Railroad Magazine* 51, no. 3 (April 1950).

Leslie, Miriam. "Gotham to the Golden Gate." *Frank Leslie's Illustrated Newspaper* (July 7, 1877).

Lo Vecchio, Janolyn G. "Allie Dickerman Brainard: Tucson's First Woman Postmaster." *The Smoke Signal,* no. 101 (March 2018).

Minter, Patricia Hagler. "The Failure of Freedom: Class, Gender, and the Evolution of Segregated Transit Law in the Nineteenth-Century South—Freedom: Personal Liberty and Private Law." *Chicago-Kent Law Review* 70, no. 3.

Paine, Charles. "The Pacific Railroad." *Godey's Lady's Book and Magazine* LXXIX, no. 470 (August 1869).

Putnam, Nina Wilcox. "The Harvey Girls—Tamers of the Wild West." *American Weekly Magazine* (August 15, 1948).

Sommers, Arthur, and Roger Staab. "Twelve Golden Years of Sara Kidder." *Nevada County Historical Society Bulletin* (1946).

Stamp, Jimmy. "Traveling in Style and Comfort: The Pullman Sleeping Car." *Smithsonian Magazine* (December 11, 2013).

Welke, Barbara Y. "When All the Women Were White, and All the Blacks Were Men: Gender, Class, Race, and the Road to Plessy, 1855–1914." *Law & History Review* 13, no. 2 (Fall 1995).

Young, Dwight. "Seeing It, Saving It: What Happens When History Comes Alive." *Preservation Magazine* (July/August 1997).

NEWSPAPERS

Albuquerque Citizen, May 10, 1902

Albuquerque Citizen, August 19, 1911

Albuquerque Journal, June 21, 1910

Albuquerque Journal, November 16, 1911

Albuquerque Journal, November 19, 1911

Albuquerque Journal, February 20, 1927

Albuquerque Journal, February 6, 1928

Alexandria Gazette (Alexandria, VA), December 10, 1897

American Weekly (New York, NY), August 15, 1948

Anaconda Standard (Anaconda, MT), July 10, 1901

Anaconda Standard (Anaconda, MT), December 12, 1901

Arizona Daily Star (Tucson), July 14, 1927

Arizona Daily Star (Tucson), May 20, 1930

Arizona Daily Sun (Flagstaff), April 6, 1955

Asbury Park Press (Neptune, NJ), February 10, 2002

Arizona Republic (Phoenix), July 24, 1911

Arizona Republic (Phoenix), June 20, 1927

Arizona Republican (Phoenix), May 15, 1930

Atchison Daily Globe (Atchison, KS), November 6, 1914

Atchison Daily Globe (Atchison, KS), July 2, 1916

Atlanta Constitution, August 17, 1930

Bakersfield Californian, October 25, 1892

Bakersfield Daily Report (Bakersfield, CA), August 2, 1905

Baltimore Sun, November 7, 1957

Baltimore Sun, May 17, 1869

Bristol Daily Courier (Bristol, PA), October 17, 1959

Buffalo Sunday Morning News (Buffalo, NY), January 11, 1903

Butte Daily Post (Butte, MT), December 13, 1901

Capital Journal (Topeka, KS), November 30, 1901

Carlsbad Current-Argus (Carlsbad, NM), February 10, 1928

Charlotte Observer (Charlotte, NC), March 30, 1916

Chicago Tribune, April 13, 1877

Chicago Tribune, February 21, 1888

Chicago Tribune, October 27, 1905

Chillicothe Constitution-Tribune (Chillicothe, MO), May 18, 1933

Cincinnati Enquirer, August 25, 1882

Clovis-News Journal (Clovis, NM), April 8, 1940

Colorado Springs Gazette-Telegraph, March 23, 1972

Courier Journal (Louisville, KY), November 29, 1881

Cuba Review (Cuba, MO), November 20, 1903

Cumberland Evening Times (Cumberland, MD), November 7, 1957

Daily Advertiser (Lafayette, LA), July 3, 1952

Daily Item (Lewisburg, PA), December 24, 2017

Daily Republican (Monongahela, PA), October 24, 1929

Dayton Daily News (Dayton, OH), July 20, 1928

Dayton Daily News (Dayton, OH), May 19, 1933

Deming Headlight (Deming, NM), December 17, 1909

Deming Headlight (Deming, NM), October 14, 2004

Denton Record Chronicle (Denton, TX), August 27, 1937
Desert News (Salt Lake, UT), May 2, 1877
Des Moines Tribune, November 20, 1968
Detroit Free Press, March 15, 1912
Dodge City Kansas Journal, March 27, 1913
Dodge City Kansas Journal, January 1, 1915
El Paso Herald, March 14, 1912
El Paso Herald-Post, October 21, 1961
El Paso Times, May 29, 1923
El Paso Times, September 24, 2000
Emporium Gazette (Emporium, KS), February 1, 1937
Evening Herald (Klamath Falls, OR), November 2, 1911
Evening Herald (Klamath Falls, OR), January 1, 1922
Evening Messenger (Marshall, TX), February 27, 1893
Evening Sun (Hanover, PA), February 24, 1921
Evening Times Republican (Marshalltown, IA), November 18, 1901
Galveston Daily News, February 7, 1904
Gazette (Cedar Rapids, IA), February 19, 1952
Great Falls Tribune (Great Falls, MT), July 4, 1901
Great Falls Tribune (Great Falls, MT), November 7, 1918
Greeley Daily Tribune (Greeley, CO), November 6, 1975
Green Bay Press-Gazette (Green Bay, WI), November 28, 1902
Indianapolis Star, January 27, 1946
Inter Ocean (Chicago, IL), December 8, 1901
Inter Ocean (Chicago, IL), March 6, 1912
Ironton County Register (Ironton, MO), July 11, 1901
Janesville Gazette (Janesville, WI), June 9, 1868
Kansas City Journal-Post (Kansas City, MO), February 29, 1897
Leader-Telegram (Eau Claire, WI), May 22, 1947
Leavenworth Times (Leavenworth, KS), February 12, 1901
Leavenworth Times (Leavenworth, KS), June 22, 1905
Leavenworth Times (Leavenworth, KS), October 19, 1917
LeRoy Reporter (LeRoy, KS), April 29, 1882
Los Angeles Herald, May 6, 1888
Los Angeles Times, November 8, 1901
Los Angeles Times, November 7, 1919
Los Angeles Times, August 20, 1924
Los Angeles Times, May 5, 1958
Louisville Bulletin (Louisville, KY), September 13, 1881
Minneapolis Journal, November 8, 1901
Morning Call (Allentown, PA), May 27, 1938

Morning Call (Allentown, PA), May 5, 1939

Morning Journal-Courier (New Haven, CT), August 13, 1885

Muncie Evening Press (Muncie, IN), September 11, 1926

Neosho Daily News (Neosho, MO), June 30, 1942

Nevada State Journal (Reno, NV), March 4, 1933

Nevada State Journal (Reno, NV), August 31, 1939

Nevada State Journal (Reno, NV), October 29, 1952

Nevada State Journal (Reno, NV), September 29, 1953

Nevada State Journal (Reno, NV), October 2, 1953

New York Herald, July 9, 1922

Newark Advocate (Newark, NJ), January 10, 1947

Oakdale Leader (Oakdale, CA), September 20, 1901

Oakland Tribune (Oakland, CA), June 28, 1910

Oakland Tribune (Oakland, CA), April 12, 1942

Ogden Standard (Ogden, UT), December 12, 1901

Ogden Standard (Ogden, UT), May 29, 1915

Oregon Daily Journal (Portland, OR), March 20, 1910

Oshkosh Northwestern (Oshkosh, WI), October 20, 1906

Ottumwa Tri-Weekly Courier (Ottumwa, IA), July 8, 1905

Palm Beach Post (Palm Beach, FL), March 2, 1947

Parsons Daily Eclipse (Parsons, KS), February 23, 1893

Philadelphia Inquirer, December 28, 1909

Philadelphia Inquirer, March 29, 1945

Pittsburgh Evening Chronicle, August 8, 1861

Pittsburgh Post, December 30, 2002

Pittsburgh Sun Telegraph, April 27, 1940

Pittsburgh Sun Telegraph, May 29, 1941

Press Tribune (Roseville, CA), October 27, 1995

Press Tribune (Roseville, CA), April 30, 1999

Province (Vancouver, BC), April 3, 1906

Ravalli Republic (Hamilton, MT), May 10, 1899

Reading Times (Reading, PA), April 20, 1882

Reno Gazette-Journal (Reno, NV), May 29, 1877

Reno Gazette-Journal (Reno, NV), November 9, 1955

Republic (Columbus, IN), February 27, 1912

Riverside Daily Press (Riverside, CA), July 10, 1886

Rutland Daily Herald (Rutland, VT), July 15, 1876

Saint Paul Globe (Saint Paul, MN), July 27, 1901

Saint Paul Globe (Saint Paul, MN), November 16, 1901

Salina Daily Union (Salina, KS), January 19, 1922

Salt Lake Tribune (Salt Lake City, UT), February 10, 1910

San Angelo Press (San Angelo, TX), November 15, 1901
San Antonio Light (San Antonio, TX), October 20, 1882
San Bernardino County Sun (San Bernardino, CA), May 22, 1933
San Bernardino County Sun (San Bernardino, CA), April 27, 1990
San Francisco Bulletin, July 8, 1908
San Francisco Call, April 11, 1901
San Francisco Call, June 14, 1901
San Francisco Call, February 17, 1907
San Francisco Call, April 10, 1913
San Francisco Call, May 11, 1913
San Francisco Call Chronicle Examiner, May 4, 1906
San Francisco Chronicle, November 10, 1908
San Francisco Chronicle, March 8, 1914
San Francisco Chronicle, March 27, 1914
San Francisco Examiner, May 7, 1869
San Francisco Examiner, April 18, 1877
San Francisco Examiner, August 14, 1881
San Francisco Examiner, December 14, 1913
San Francisco Examiner, September 30, 1933
San Francisco Examiner, March 19, 1949
San Francisco Examiner, July 31, 1955
Santa Fe New Mexican, January 23, 1911
Santa Fe New Mexican, March 12, 1978
Santa Maria Times (Santa Maria, CA), March 8, 1877
Seguin Gazette Enterprise (Seguin, TX), December 14, 1914
Seguin Gazette Enterprise (Seguin, TX), December 14, 1994
Southern Illinoisan (Carbondale, IL), October 18, 1971
Spirit of the Age (Woodstock, VT), July 26, 1876
Spokane Chronicle (Spokane, WA), July 8, 1901
Springville Journal (East Aurora, NY), September 28, 1878
St. Joseph Gazette-Herald (St. Joseph, MO), April 12, 1888
St. Louis Post-Dispatch, June 12, 1904
St. Louis Post-Dispatch, September 21, 1905
St. Louis Post-Dispatch, December 29, 1952
St. Louis Republic, November 8, 1901
St. Louis Star & Times, January 17, 1911
Standard Union (Brooklyn, NY), October 27, 1905
Star Democrat (Easton, MD), January 17, 1947
Star Gazette (Elmira, NY), October 19, 1914
Star Press (Muncie, IN), October 6, 1963
Statesman Journal (Salem, OR), May 15, 1900

Statesman Journal (Salem, OR), November 30, 1901
Statesman Journal (Salem, OR), December 23, 2001
Tacoma Times (Tacoma, WA), September 2, 1913
Tallahassee Democrat (Tallahassee, FL), January 28, 1963
Tampa Tribune (Tampa, FL), December 30, 1952
Telegrapher (New York), July 15, 1876
Telegrapher (New York), September 23, 1876
Times (New York), December 18, 1877
Times (New York), May 7, 1900
Times (New York), May 30, 1937
Times (New York), April 24, 1939
Times Tribune (Corbin, KY), June 23, 1921
Topeka Daily Capital, March 22, 1890
Topeka Daily Capital, July 4, 1909
Topeka Standard, July 15, 1922
Utah Daily Union (Ogden City, UT), June 12, 1888
Washington Post (Washington, DC), December 4, 1908
Weekly Davenport Democrat (Davenport, IA), April 26, 1877
Wichita Beacon (Wichita, KS), December 10, 1897

WEBSITES

https://alchetron.com/Julia-Bulette
www.ancestry.com
http://calzephyr.railfan.net
http://digital.library.pitt.edu/u/ulmanuscripts/pdf/3175061545012.pdf
https://www.econedlink.org/wp-content/uploads/legacy/719_railroads1.pdf
https://www.engineergirl.org/125278/Olive-Dennis
http://www.hevac-heritage.org/built_environment/biographies/surnames_M-
    R/pennington/P1-PENNINGTON.pdf
https://www.kshs.org/kansapedia/fred-harvey/15507
http://moorewomenartists.org/philadelphia
www.nationalrailroadhalloffame.org
http://prototyperails.com/PDF/Abstracts_rev04_2019.pdf
https://www.researchgate.net/publication/35007244_The_order_of_railroad_
    telegraphers_a_study_in_trade_unionism_and_collective_bargaining
https://santafeselection.com/blog/2014/06/21/Indian-detours-now

INDEX

About the Author

Chris Enss is a *New York Times* best-selling author who has been writing about women of the Old West for more than twenty years. She has penned more than forty published books on the subject. Her book titled *Entertaining Ladies: Actresses, Singers, and Dancers in the Old West* was a Spur Award finalist in 2017. Enss's book *Mochi's War: The Tragedy of the Sand Creek Massacre* received the Will Rogers Medallion Award for best nonfiction Western for 2015. Her book titled *Object Matrimony: The Risky Business of Mail Order Matchmaking on the Western Frontier* won the Elmer Kelton Award for Best Nonfiction book of 2013. Enss's book *Sam Sixkiller: Frontier Cherokee Lawman* was named Outstanding Book on Oklahoma History by the Oklahoma Historical Society.